MY BARGAIN WITH GOD

The Story of Holocaust Survivor LOU DUNST

By **BEN KAMIN**

Afterword by **ALBERTO HAMUI**

My Bargain With God: The Story of Holocaust Survivor Lou Dunst
Copyright © 2014 by Lou Dunst and Alberto Hamui
All rights reserved. First edition 2014

Edited by S. L. Kay
Cover design by Keren Dee Hamui
Cover photograph is used courtesy of Robert Schneider and Alberto Lau Photography
Book design by Michael Schrauzer
Project management by Deborah Young
Production by Sunbelt Publications, Inc.
Printed in the United States of America

Please direct comments and inquiries to:
Alberto Hamui
info@loudunst.com

18 17 16 15 14   5 4 3 2 1

Library of Congress Cataloging-in-Publication Data

Kamin, Ben.
  My bargain with God the story of Holocaust survivor Lou Dunst / by Ben
Kamin ; afterword by Alberto Hamui. -- First edition.
     pages cm
  ISBN 978-0-916251-44-4 (alk. paper)
  1. Dunst, Lou, 1926- 2. Jews--Czechoslovakia--Biography. 3. Holocaust
survivors--Biography I. Title.
  DS135.C97D865 2014
  940.53'18092--dc23
  [B]
                        2013047987

TO THE BLESSED MEMORY
of my mother and father, Priva and Mordecai,
who vanished in Auschwitz; to my sister Risi,
who suffered for decades the consequences
of the Holocaust; and to my brother Irving,
my other self, my window to life; and to the
six million of our Jewish brothers' and sisters'
souls, victims that were reduced to ashes
during the biggest catastrophe of mankind.

NEVER AGAIN.

—*Lou Dunst*

ACKNOWLEDGMENTS

My *Bargain With God* IS NOT ONLY THE TITLE OF THIS BOOK BUT it is also my pact—my personal Brit—that has shaped the last seventy years of my existence. Every day, every moment of my life has been geared to spread the word to the rest of the world about the Holocaust, the worst man-made catastrophe of the human race. Every generation must learn about how intolerance, hatred and violence lead to the mass murder of six million Jewish men, women and children so that it shall not happen again.

I have not been alone in fulfilling my part of *My Bargain With God*. In deed I have been very fortunate to receive guidance and help from a number of individuals that I warmly and respectfully call branches of my tree of life. The roots of that tree were my parents and siblings from which my trunk was formed. There are no words I can express my gratitude for their deep influence in my upbringing.

The first and the most important branch is my friend and love life companion wife Estelle. She has been the one that has always helped me to speak out my history. She encouraged me almost thirty years ago to my first, and then, to the many thousands of the talks I have performed in front of a variety of different audiences. She is the one behind the scenes that inspired the writing of this book.

Probably one of the thickest branches in the tree is my love of the Torah. Growing from that branch, I have been fortunate to meet several knowledgeable and spiritual rabbis and cantors who helped me shape my tree. The branch of one of them, Rabbi and Soffer Alberto Attia, has illuminated and added color to the way I see the Torah. Thank you from the bottom of my heart.

A couple of branches that were of great influence on the development of my tree were Judge Janet Berry from Reno, Nevada and Federal Judge

Norbert Ehrenfreund from San Diego, California. They guided and advised me, and I am grateful to them from the bottom of my heart.

When I accepted to cooperate for the writing of this book the journey started with the need to find an experienced writer who would have the sensitivity and knowledge of the values and history of the Jewish people. We found those attributes and more in Ben Kamin. As another important branch, he was immersed in the history and the everyday of my life. What he enthused into the book was beyond any duty. The contributions to this book by my editor S.L. Kay, a branch whom I gracefully call her Koba, have been substantial and very much appreciated. I am grateful to both of them from the bottom of my heart.

An unexpected branch started to grow as volunteers Bob Schneider and "Albie" Lau graphically documented the making and the history of this book. Thanks to their research and commitment we have copies of photographs taken by the liberators of my last concentration camp. Those photographs are contained in this book and they have never been released to the public before. Also, they have a huge volume of video interviews documented and catalogued that will be available for the present and the future generations. Thank you both from the bottom of my heart.

Branches and more branches developed during the last few months from a lot of volunteers: Michal Hamui has been helping and contributing ideas to this journey since its inception; her son Teddy and daughter-in-law Keren Dee Hamui are helping to incorporate the message of this book through the Internet, offering to develop and host LouDunst.com to promote and expand my Jewish moral values. More volunteered branches appeared when Michal formed a Committee together with Reina Shteremberg, Vanina Bunton, Estelle, Keren Dee, Monica Bauer, Morris Casuto, Jacky Gmach and others, to help spread the message of *My Bargain With God*. To all of them, and to all of the other branches that are sprouting every day: thank you, thank you from the very bottom of my heart.

My Tree has come into full maturity and the branches are all blossoming with the completion of this book. This is all due to the endless and meticulous work of Alberto Hamui who with the assistance of Michal and their family put together every aspect and page of my story. They made all arrangements and assumed all of the responsibilities for publishing. I am deeply grateful to Alberto and Michal for achieving this goal. They put aside many personal, business and family matters to complete this project. Ha-Shem has blessed me to bring my best friend, Alberto into my life.

—*Lou Dunst*

ORIGINAL PAINTING COURTESY OF EDDY COHEN H.

AUTHOR ACKNOWLEDGMENTS

I AM GRATEFUL TO MORRIS CASUTO, THE LONGTIME DIRECTOR OF the San Diego regional office of the Anti-Defamation League. Morris invited me to lunch one day and told me that a remarkable man, a survivor of the Nazi Holocaust, and a widely-traveled chronicler of his own passage through it, had acceded to others' wishes that his story be converted into a book.

This wonderful meeting led to a second session, this time with Alberto Hamui of San Diego. It turns out that Alberto, an elegant and sincerely spiritual man, had been looking after Lou Dunst's chronicle for many years. He had accumulated video recordings made in his own office and elsewhere, photos, notes, and endless mementos of an astonishing journey and survival.

More importantly for Alberto, he worshipped weekly with Lou in a local synagogue, deeply affected and moved by the spiritual bond that immediately developed and grew between them. It was Alberto who finally convinced Lou, after years of persuasion, that "The Book" must be written.

I first met Lou, appropriately, in that synagogue. He was, as always, totally himself. His business in the "shull" was to mingle with God and heal his soul. Yet he was not aloof or distant. He took me into his heart without any declarations and, to my relief, accepted me with the quiet glow of his very knowledgeable eyes.

Though I shudder to make any comparisons with Lou's experience, he'd be the first to allow me the analogy: Thank you, good God, for letting me live, so that I could tell Lou's story.

—*Ben Kamin*
Encinitas, California
November 30, 2013

TABLE OF CONTENTS

	Dedication	*v*
	Acknowledgments	*vii*
	Author Acknowledgments	*x*
CHAPTER ONE	*"We could not see the sun"*	1
CHAPTER TWO	*"It was in their mother's milk"*	11
CHAPTER THREE	*Three Torah Scrolls*	21
CHAPTER FOUR	*A Trail of Suffering*	37
CHAPTER FIVE	*The Cookie Factory*	45
CHAPTER SIX	*"Like the Stars in The Heaven"*	55
CHAPTER SEVEN	*"The Staircase of Death"*	65
CHAPTER EIGHT	*"We have to stay away from the cruelty"*	77
CHAPTER NINE	*"My name is Israel"*	85
CHAPTER TEN	*"How would I have behaved?"*	95
CHAPTER ELEVEN	*"The Sisters of Mercy"*	103
CHAPTER TWELVE	*"Rome was a crossroads"*	113
CHAPTER THIRTEEN	*"We can pray anywhere!"*	121
CHAPTER FOURTEEN	*Last Rites from a Catholic Priest*	129
CHAPTER FIFTEEN	*"It was time for Lou to have a birthday"*	135
AFTERWORD	*"Lou's Love of Life's Moral Values"*	143
	Photo Gallery	151

CHAPTER ONE

"We could not see the sun"
Ebensee Death Camp, Austria
May 6, 1945

NUMBER 68122 STRUGGLED AGAINST THE STINKING MOUNTAIN OF corpses wedged against him, above him, and beneath him. He barely noticed the searing stench; it was something he was accustomed to, a fact of subsistence as constant as his unyielding preparation for death. He choked against lifeless heads, shrunken breasts, unmoving limbs as sharp-edged from malnutrition and typhoid and pestilence as his own mind was blurred with fear and confusion. With each gasping gulp of foul air, a vague internal weaving of Hebrew letters somehow rose from the pyre in a fume.

There was no sky above 68122, no earth below, no sun, wind, and certainly no singing of birds. He was completely naked against the similarly bare, rotting, broken bits of former human lives that accumulated about him on what was certain to be his final moments among endless days. 68122 had no comprehension of what day it actually was on the calendar—even examining a calendar or just noting the time of day/night it was unthinkable. Any relationship with the clock had yielded to an unyielding desolation.

His throat burned from ashes, his lips peeled from dehydration, his stomach churned with hunger and nausea, his teeth rattled like loose gravel, and his fingernails were black and shattered from slave labor and filth. He shrank from the vultures that swooped around and beneath him, "doing their job" as he thought fitfully to himself.

Blinking his hollow eyes against the heap of death, 68122 tried to think about the green hills and beech trees and limestone rocks of the Carpathian Mountains of his childhood. He would gaze at the arcing snowcapped peaks, the sharp descent of the pined carpet valleys, and take in the scent of bellflowers, violets, and primroses. The alpine crests were a relief to the somewhat dreary, all-too-often dangerous realities of his boyhood; Jew-hating bullies and menacing magistrates and hostile church priests were all a staple of life. When the mountain winds finally brought with them the SS and the murderous, machine gun-toting *Einsatzgruppen* (select army squads deployed to shoot Jews), all a prelude to the deportations, the ghettos, and finally to the death camps, it was but the culmination of a long bad dream that lingered at the margins of Jewish existence in that part of the world.

But still, 68122, in actuality a human being named Lou Israel Dunst, grimaced in concentration and prayer and, somehow, the faintest glimmer of hope. He was a so-called *muselmann*—a person so named because he had no flesh on his bones and was no longer able to walk or even stand up. But Lou still had a faintly beating heart, and a will to transcend the bacteria, the parasites, the welts, the hideous cruelty and neglect of his SS masters.

Far from him, other things were happening across the blood-soaked landscape of Europe of May 6, 1945. In Holland, one of so many nations brutalized into submission by the now-crumbling Third Reich, General Johannes Albrecht Blaskowitz , recipient of the Knight's Cross of the Iron Cross, surrendered his troops to Canadian forces. Across the continent, similar submissions were occurring; the war that took some 59 million lives, from Gibraltar to Siberia, from Normandy to Norway, was finally ending. On the same day that 68122 was groping for life on a pile of death, the notorious "Axis Sally" (Mildred Gillars) delivered her final propaganda broadcast from Berlin; she had been profaning the air waves and maligning US troops, in perfect English since December 11, 1941 and would soon be arrested for treason. The war in Europe officially ended on May 8, but the outside world had no impact today on 68122 as he pleaded with God in a haze of rotting mortality and clinging faith.

Recalling a terse devotion from his days in Hebrew School back in Jasina, Czechoslovakia, 68122 faintly nodded his head and whispered to himself, "Let me live, Lord, so that I may tell the story…."

At that same moment, a convoy of military vehicles and foot soldiers, the Third Cavalry, was entering the massive industrial complex of Ebensee, eyeing the quarries and noticing the gaping tunnel entrances that had been constructed by Jewish slaves for the past several years. They would learn from the shattered survivors inside that the burrows and caverns underneath the industrialized camp—a subterranean grid of bondage and horror—were lined with heavy explosives. The manifold thousand inmates were well-drilled via the orders of camp *Kommandmant* SS Obersturmfuhrer Anton Ganz, a man Lou Dunst would describe as "the top beast."

Historical records show that the following methods were employed by

Ganz and his henchmen to achieve their parallel goals of having their slaves construct the underground factories and mass produce military hardware within them—with no consideration to human life whatsoever:

In lieu of the gas chambers that many of the Ebensee inmates had somehow eluded (this having happened twice to Lou Dunst), starvation was the most commonly relied-upon mode for killing the helpless and destitute workers. Lou had a bracelet with the number 68122 stamped upon it. His brother Irving, who was also in Ebensee, had the successive bracelet numbered 68123. Neither Lou nor Irving, two years his senior, carried the trademark number-tattoos of the concentration camps—even though they had both previously endured Auschwitz. The two brothers, who saw each other intermittently, carried each other's spirits. The Nazis had chosen not to waste the ink required to burn numbers onto the flesh of the teenage boys because, as they were gleefully assured many times by SS officers: "Don't worry, there is no need for you to have a tattoo because you are going to the gas chamber anyway."

The Germans, grisly efficient, gathered the used casings of the deadly Zyklon-B gas cans, the main toxin of the gas chambers, to make the numbered bracelets for Lou and Irving and the untold thousands and thousands of other such victims.

Other procedures used by Ganz at Ebensee to dispose of their prisoners included the reliance upon disease, unthinkable sanitation, exposure to the elements, and even the inevitable suicides of inmates made deranged by their experience. The SS also threw helpless workers against high voltage electrical fences or they simply strangled, fatally beat, or just shot workers who could no longer deal with the horror, could not carry the daily dead bodies back to camp (to maintain the daily count of prisoners), or did not respond properly or immediately to the barking commands of their guards.

Sometimes, vicious, trained dogs were dispatched to tear a person into pieces; other inmates were expected to promptly clean up the bloody parts and fleshy ravages or face immediate extermination themselves. The Germans used gunfire from towers, knives, or their bare hands to kill off prisoners who were no longer of use.

One historian has documented another practice that Lou and Irving witnessed all too often in Ebensee: those individuals not able to work and erect armament factories were thrown into tied sacks and then beaten to death with clubs.

By May 6, 1945, *Kommandmant* Ganz had another major plan in place with respect to his charges. 68122, Lou Dunst, actually heard Ganz' deceitful speech a few days prior: the Allies were approaching and he, Ganz, wanted to protect the prisoners. Upon his order, they would be gathered to safety within the underground complexes of the camp. The tunnel's entranceway, however, had actually been lined with explosives. Irving Dunst knew about this because he, being a little stronger and broader than his little brother, and with some experience as a driller, worked in that area. He told Lou and both trembled with the lie and with the certainty of being buried alive in the mass grave for over 16,000 people.

The SS plan was simple: should Allied troops breach the compound, the prisoners were to be immediately directed into the tunnels and the dynamite set to go off so that they and the truth would be consumed. The civilians from nearby villages along Lake Traun would be recruited, handed daggers and rifles, to help organize and drag the inmates to their tomb. The sudden discovery of the camp by the Third Army prevented this diabolical final act from happening.

In fact, the combat-weary group had been on general patrol in the area, seeking out scurrying Nazi troops—the killing camp was more or less stumbled upon. The men were about to see and experience something they had not even seen in the most gruesome battle zones.

The foul air was filled with murder and contaminants. A few skeletal beings, the carnage of Europe, unclothed and barely able to move, were seen bowed against broken railings or over rusty barrels. Most of them had long lost the pathetic wooden clogs they had originally been given; they had been barefoot in the Austrian winters for what seemed like an eternity. When it was possible, they were forced to subsist upon morning food rations consisting of half a liter of ersatz coffee; at noon, three-quarters of a liter of hot water containing potato peelings; in the evening, 150 grams of bread.

The GIs, a contingent of General George S. Patton's Third Army, were just beginning to comprehend what they could not imagine and what they would never forget. Nor would its residue ever truly leave their nostrils. The smell of piled corpses, intensified by urine and feces, was intolerable. Nor would their eyes erase the image of what one of them described as "a mass of shrunken, ghastly scarecrows." Lou Dunst would tell people over the years that "they could not believe their own eyes. They could not even believe their own cameras."

They noticed that, but for two sentries at the gate who were quickly detained, one brandishing a rifle and the other a bazooka, there were no German soldiers, no guards, and no evidence of the sentinels who had pitilessly overseen this ghoulish place. In fact, Ganz and his men had fled the night before. [Anton Ganz successfully hid under a false name in Austria and was not arrested by West German authorities until 1967.]

In one tank, GI Robert Persinger literally drove through the camp fence, which gave way like dry straw against the force of American armor. Persinger, a lanky Iowa farm boy, was a 21-year-old sergeant in the Third Cavalry Reconnaissance Group. He commanded the lead tank that broke down the gates of the dreaded concentration camp. His vehicle, named "Lady Luck," was seen by a few of the remaining inmates; they recognized the possibility of freedom via the solitary white American star emblazoned across its hulk. Persinger emerged in his dark olive uniform—a mighty figure with muscle tone as against the wasted, dazed semi-figures that happened to alight along Lady Luck's path. The sky was sunny above the tangled mess of bondage and freedom.

Persinger remembers the scene:

> As we approached on the gravel road to the camp, we saw masses of human beings that appeared almost as ghosts standing in mud and filth up to their ankles behind the high wire fence. None of us had ever seen human beings in this terrible situation before. We started to toss rations and energy bars to them until our supply was depleted. The stench of the dead bodies was almost unbearable. We went to the crematorium, where there were stacks of bodies piled like cordwood. If you weren't sick by now, you would be before you left. At the same time, you wanted to cry.

He added: "We had seen terrible sights in combat across Europe but this was beyond anyone's imagination."

The scene of human blight was so gruesome that the soldiers were initially reluctant to emerge from their armored vehicles. Hardened troops of blood and gore, they were afraid of the contagions to their own bodies these bewildered *muselmann* figures could pass onto them. Robert Persinger, now ninety years old and living in Illinois, recalled for the author, his voice intermittently cracking with emotion:

> There were about ten of us, in four tanks. I couldn't believe what we were looking at. We pulled in and we turned off the engines

in our tanks and we talked to one another among the tanks, by radio. We didn't want to get out and down among that mass of dying, starving human beings, you know, so filthy, it was so terrible. And we had never seen anything like that in our lives. Anyway, I leaned back and got a cigarette ... there happened to be a carton of Lucky Strikes. A man along the side of our tank said out loud, "It's been a long time since I've had a Lucky Strike." So that man was looking up and I said, "Well, just come up to the tank and I'll give you one." He could understand English. He was about the only guy who could speak English that day. I mean, there were all kinds of languages. I was so surprised. He was stronger that most of them, he had a little more meat on his bones than most of them—a little more.... His father, mother, and sister were gassed in Auschwitz. He was young enough and strong enough to convince them to keep him alive. He helped them build buildings, he was an architect. This fella convinced us to come down from the tanks. He wanted to walk us around and show us the camp. That is why, while Lou Dunst was lying in the crematorium, which I didn't know of course at that moment, that's why we went into the place.

First we went into the kitchen area there, and we went through the barracks. And that was so sickening, the barracks smelled so terrible. And from the minute we got off the tanks, well they were all over us. They wanted us to lift them and help them. Those poor people, they were so thrilled to see someone who was on their side.... When we got past the barracks and into the crematorium we were crying. Bodies lying around, ready to be burned, naked.... What an initiation for us.

The soldiers turned to the basic need glaringly in evidence: starvation. Persinger and his crew started confiscating food supplies; some of the soldiers were quickly dispatched to the nearby village where they gathered large kettles. They had no patience for townspeople who tried to withhold their pots and pans and they brandished their tank guns whenever someone tried to resist. They were shockingly aware that every second could spell the difference for the people they had just seen who were dying in front of them.

In Ebensee, the soldiers prepared huge vats of steaming thick soup for the ravenous camp inmates. Some of the prisoners had been subsisting on snatched pieces of charcoal. A number did not survive even those initial hours of liberation day; others tasted the beginnings of new life as the young men from Iowa, South Carolina, Minnesota, and New York ladle-fed them, spoke to them, held them up, and began to sort them out for medical evacuation.

Now, Irving Dunst, suddenly the former #68123, grabbed the arm of a random soldier in Sergeant Persinger's detachment. Irving was ashen and dizzy and the GI at first did not realize that a human being was actually tugging at him. Irving pulled the GI a bit and directed him to one of the piles of bodies left rotting in the sun by the fleeing Germans. Irving jabbed his finger in the air, clearly pointing at one of the figures at the top of the heap. It was 68122. "That's my brother!" cried Irving Dunst. "Please rescue him."

68122, Lou Israel Dunst, lingered at the edge of death, but he was still alive. Lou, gravely diseased, with hardly a pulse, and with a last prayer, had not died. "We are liberated!" cried Irving into the yellowed ear of his faint brother. Lou pulled pack and withheld from eternity what would have been his last breath. Like a vague, soothing mist from his childhood in Jasina , sitting in the cramped *cheyder* (Hebrew School) with the other Jewish students, an old, familiar prayer crept into his pounding head: *Lo amoot, ki echye....* "I shall not die but live so that I can tell of the doings of God." For Lou, "this was my bargaining with God." He whispered it as: "I shall not die but live to tell the story."

As a result, the world would not be permitted to ever forget what had happened to him, his brother, his sister, their parents—who had been vaporized at Auschwitz—and to the other millions of Jewish fathers, mothers, husbands, wives, and little children in what Lou Dunst has told thousands of people over the last seven decades was "the greatest criminal act ever committed in the history of mankind."

This book is not the story of the evil, although it is impossible to write the book without recalling the evil and horror and insanity of the Nazi genocide of the Jewish people that took place ("while the nations did nothing," says Lou Dunst) between 1933 and 1945. Nor, as Lou reminds us, was there a shortage of anti-Semitism and violence against Jewish lives before Adolf Hitler took power in Germany in 1933. There were also bloody spasms of organized brutality against Jews in the years following the official close of the war. Irving and Lou personally suffered from intimidation and beatings, in scattered towns and while clinging to the tops of trains, as they desperately tried to make their way back to their Carpathian home after liberation—only to discover years later that their home was no longer theirs.

Many centuries of institutional Jew-hatred, pogroms, segregation, and dehumanization, authorized by church leaders and legislated by states, created a deadly viral context of mass murder that culminated at the instigation of the Third Reich. The three children of Priva and Mordecai Dunst (Risi, Irving, and Lou), grew up with institutionalized prejudice, bias, and violence directed at them. "I never remember any time," says Lou, "when we were not down."

And yet, this book is about love. It is the small scripture, the little Talmud of a physically unimposing man, somewhat cherubic, vulnerable, with a soft tone and polite manners, who speaks to individuals and to groups around the world, in an irresistible voice tinged with the accent of both faraway places and close-to-the-vest pain. This is the testimony of a man who admits to regular nightmares but lives to dream of hope in the daytime.

Standing there without notes, in conference rooms, at synagogue pulpits, church lecterns, and in gymnasiums, wearing a yarmulke on his graying head that looks like a little angelic beanie, his eyes brimming with both kindness and conviction, the man silences a crowd of normally inattentive junior high school students, grasps the attention of Navy Seals, Lions Club members, physicians and judges, and shames a smattering of skinheads with the simple facts of his unbearably unique story and his untiring faith in *"Ha-Shem"*—God. Policemen weep, nuns pray, rabbis are overwhelmed, mothers and fathers renew their holds on their kids, and hardened journalists melt in the light of Lou Israel Dunst.

"I did nothing special and nothing heroic to survive," he says. "My brother saved me. We were united. He was the stronger one. The only thing I did was keep my faith in *Ha-Shem*. I bargained with him. Somehow I felt that God was even in the boxcars, where people were piled up, 100 in a car, sweltering, nothing to drink, nothing to eat, no toilet facilities. We had nothing. Nothing! This one died, this one relieved himself, that one gave birth. We could not see the sun. But still I believed. My name is Israel. That is my name. What would happen if we will all be murdered and nobody will be able to tell about it? *Ha-Shem* saved me to tell the story. I'm grateful for every single breath I take. I think about every bite of food I'm privileged to eat. What could I talk about with the other prisoner? He was cold, I was cold. He was hungry, I was hungry. He missed his parents, I missed my parents. What could we really talk about?

The point is to talk about it now so it shouldn't happen again. We have to love each other. We are all God's children. We have to stop with the hatreds. You don't like the way that one parts his hair, so what? You don't like the sound of that one's accent—so what? For this we should kill each other? There should be no hatreds. There should be no animosity. I am obligated to tell the story to you. I will tell it to one person; I will tell it to five hundred. I am trying to clean my heart. There is no hatred in my heart, only love. *Baruch ha-Shem.* Blessed be the name of God."

This book is the little hymnal, the manual of ethics, which has been taught by Lou Dunst, from a pile of the dead in Ebensee via Czechoslovakia and Italy and Canada and to the children of the United States. This is his book of life, the documentation of his fulfilled bargain with God.

CORPSES TAKEN FROM THE EBENSEE CREMATORIA TO A PROPER BURIAL.
(PHOTO TAKEN BY ROBERT PERSINGER'S BRIGADE, MAY 6, 1945)

Give thanks to the Lord, for He is good;
His love endures forever.
Let Israel say:
"His love endures forever."
When hard pressed, I cried to the Lord;
He brought me into a spacious place.
The Lord is with me; I will not be afraid.
What can mere mortals do to me?
The Lord is with me; He is my helper.
I look in triumph on my enemies.
The Lord's right hand is lifted high;
the Lord's right hand has done mighty things!"
I shall not die but live,
and will proclaim what the Lord has done.
This is the gate of the Lord
through which the righteous may enter.
I will give You thanks, for You answered me;
You have become my salvation.
— from Psalm 118

CHAPTER TWO

"It was in their mother's milk"

LOU DUNST LIKES TO SAY THAT WHEN YOU ARE LOOKING AT A map of Czechoslovakia (now the Czech Republic), "You can find the Carpathian Mountains, but you can't find Jasina!" His squeaky, infectious little laugh comes through—a joyous sound that is nonetheless muffled by the facts of his life. It is the report of a man who wants very hard to relish an irony but is nonetheless disciplined by experience and courtesy ("I shouldn't make too much noise," he seems to be thinking) and not a small measure of guilt. Like most survivors of the genocide, Lou wonders a lot about why he is here and the others are not. And like the tiny village of Jasina, he often feels like an invisible spot against the highlands of history.

But the village was real, just as a number of Jewish families, never truly secure, never fully integrated socially into the community, owned wood-framed groceries and general merchandise stores and maintained kindling for their houses and a low profile for their security. "We lived in the center of the town mostly," remembers Lou. "There was really just one dirt road and then another one, sideways. The non-Jews lived along the foothills."

He was the youngest of the three children and his family called him "Lu-Lu"— an affectionate twist on the end of his given Hebrew name, Israel and according to Risi, Lou sang a song in his crib pronouncing the words "Lu-Lu", so they affectionately called him Lu-Lu, which years later became Lou. Risi, the sister, was the oldest, followed by Irving. The town was at the easternmost point of the country but that patch of Europe changed hands six times during the Twentieth Century. The realignments only reflected the unstable nature of life in the community that was particularly felt—and suffered by—the Jewish residents of the area.

Today, Jasina is a small urban town in Ukraine. According to the *"JewishGen"* web site, twenty-one Jews lived in the hamlet in 1830. There were 786 Jews there in 1877 and then the Jewish population peaked at 1,403 in 1941 within an overall population of approximately 7,000. Consistent with the Dunst family story, the Jews began to vanish quickly thereafter. A bloody starting point: in August, 1941, about 300 local Jews, some complete families, were expelled to

Kamenets-Podolski in Ukraine, where they were murdered—together with thousands of other Jews from the area—who similarly lacked Hungarian citizenship (the Hungarians had seized jurisdiction with Nazi underwriting.)

Jasina was mapped within the Hutsul Republic following World War I; a number of leading Ukrainians were born there who spearheaded the region's independence from what was then the Kingdom of Hungary. This short-lived republic was terminated when Romanian troops entered in 1919. But before that year was out, Jasina was re-occupied by Hungary. The whirlwinds following the First War already were sending the seeds of turmoil and displacement and the eventual Nazism of the Second into the groceries, tanneries, stables, blacksmith shops, and tiny Jewish grade schools of the little bitter crossroads along the peaks.

It was still 1919 when Jasina passed to Czechoslovakia. Then, in accordance with the hastily written Treaty of Trianon Hungary again occupied it from 1939 to 1944. It was absorbed by the Soviet Union in 1945 and now, post-USSR, is Ukrainian. A well-known church and steeple made of timber has withstood all of these transitions and stands in the center of town. But the Jews have not: all are gone now—they were never Hungarians, Romanians, Czechs, Poles, Russians, or Ukrainians. They were Jews.

"I have visited there many times," says Lou, his eyes narrowing with pain. "There is not one single Jew there anymore. Our house, the house I grew up in—some other family lives there."

Mordecai and Priva Dunst worked hard and expected little from life but to survive and look after their children. Their world was not about dreams; it was an extended narrative of a sometimes harsh reality. "We Jews were about twenty percent of the town," remembers Lou. There was no concept of a horizon or a better future for Jewish families, of any entitlement other than a second-class citizenship within a changing national tapestry of regimes and the perpetual church tower that rose in the center of their meager existence. The Jews with little stores, the few Jewish families who owned sawmills, and the Jews who taught other Jews—they were a civilization unto themselves more in tune with the Hebrew calendar that sustained them than the civic authorities who scorned them.

The memories of Jasina for Lou consist primarily of "unpaved roads" and "always the snow on the top of the mountains." His deepest recollection is always about the home in which he lived for the few years before the storm of genocide pulled him away and devastated his family. He always asserts: "I need to say a few things about my home. We looked after each other. There was peace there. We didn't have electricity. We didn't have running water. But we had each other. And every Friday afternoon, we had the Sabbath. We never forgot the Sabbath. Never. It kept us together."

The antagonism of the non-Jews, called "the *goyim*" (the term actually means, simply, "the nations"), was not so much a raging issue for him and the others as much as it was a given, a fact of life—like the cold wind or the thick pines that came sloping down the nearby peaks. The Jews spoke Yiddish among themselves and the Christians, mostly Greek Orthodox or Catholic spoke a Ukrainian dialect known as Hucul. It was sprinkled with Polish influences and grew out of a culture based on forestry and logging, as well as some mountain farming. Says Lou: "The soil was not a productive soil. They raised sheep and cows. The weather was hard. The *goyim* were poor. The Jews maybe less poor and we had stores where they also came to shop."

The Jews and the Ukrainians were foreigners to one another, townsfolk versus hill people. The danger, the seething animosity rose daily with sun but did not set when night came into the village. The Ukrainians had their bag pipes and hams; the Jews had their shofars and chickens. Good Friday/Easter and Passover, linked by calendar and hatred, were dangerous times for the Jews and ripe seasons for pogroms. The priests in the churches would provoke their parishioners with the slander of Jews being "Christ-killers!" Riots and vandalism broke out, Jewish homes burned, property stolen, Torah scrolls torn apart, people wounded or killed. "We just lived with it," says Lou, his shoulders sagging with the weight of history.

"We were never safe. It was already going on for generations, the pogroms. The anti-Semitism was in their mother's milk. They were born with it. They would hit us, screaming 'Beat the Jew! Save our Russia!' When it would happen, we would only say to each other, 'Thank God, it wasn't worse.' Or people would try and explain it by saying things like, 'He must have been drunk. Maybe he was just a crazy person.' We didn't understand it. We were decent people. We weren't criminals to be treated in such a way."

The Ukrainians spit at the Jews, attacked them on their way to and from school, and sometimes kidnapped their teenage boys for sale to the army. From birth, Lou and his siblings knew that the *goyim* were not their friends. Too often, he suffered blows to the head, a brick thrown at his back, a fist into his belly. Mobs sometimes inflicted severe physical damage to Jewish homes and businesses. The eruptions were encouraged and condoned by the civic authorities whose job was to keep the peace. Like bad burns, the pogroms remain a fiery fact of European history and they foreshadow the Holocaust of six million Jews, including one-and-half million children—what Lou emotionally labels "the greatest catastrophe in the history of mankind."

Yet with all this, Lou smiles and retains kind memories of his family life. Even while grieving for Priva and Mordecai, his parents, who were killed in Auschwitz, Lou focuses on life. "We had a general merchandise store. We lived in the same building as the store. We all worked together in the store, we were always a family. This is what I tell people when I speak to them now, the students, the older people, everyone. Don't ever give up the unity of the family. There is nothing like it."

That "family devotion," as Lou also terms it, gave them the determination to build a "sukkah"—the little booth constructed by Jewish families during the eight-day fall harvest festival of "Sukkot" (which means "booths.") Cold weather biting at them, they faithfully erected the deliberately frail hut, with a thatched roof, as an extension of the house. The holiday rejoices in the earth's vegetation and abundance. It connects Jews to the creation right after spending so much focusing on personal renewal through Yom Kippur. The fragile booth, bending to the wind, symbolizes our belief in God's presence and watchfulness. The roof is thatched to allow the star shine to penetrate; there is no need for security systems or high fences when you believe in heavenly providence. No one can believe in that more than Lou Dunst—that's why he talks to any one or any group that will listen about what happened to the Jews of Europe.

In spite of everything that happened to the Dunst family at the hands of the fascists and their eagerly willing cohorts in every corner of Europe, including the indescribable destruction of Jewish property, possessions, and lives, Lou still invokes his belief in a world of unsecured dwellings and peaceful homes.

Following tradition, the three Dunst children and their parents would share simple meals in the hut, shivering in the bitter weather but gathering warmth from one another. "There was snow already," Lou remembers. "But my father would bless the wine and the bread and we would welcome the spirits of our ancestors into the sukkah. We stuck close together, just like all the Jewish families."

In the spring, Passover was celebrated inside the house with the ritualistic Seder meal; no holiday was observed lacking the appropriate foods and songs and liturgies—even if the observances were sometimes interrupted by thrown rocks or invectives or even worse from the Christian townsfolk. The warm blanket of family dedication and caring; the deeply interpersonal relationships among the children and the parents—these vivid recollections are likely the reason Lou Dunst tells groups that he addresses in the 21st century to never forget the notion of familial loyalty and tenderness.

Meanwhile, the Dunst store opened every day but for the Sabbath, meaning it was shut down from Friday afternoon through Saturday night. The Sabbath transcended everything—not only the day itself, but the preparation, the scrubbing, polishing, cooking, and the excitement of rest and calm and some holy text.

On Friday mornings, Lou would breathe in the pleasing aroma of his mother baking the weekly challah—the twisted Sabbath bread that crowned the center of the table on Friday night, along with the cherished candlesticks and the cups of sweet kosher red wine. "You know," he reminisced, "on the Sabbath, everything was cleaned. Every week we looked forward to it. The town streets were so often muddy. So on Friday, we would go down to the river and wash our shoes from the mud. Everything had to be clean for the Sabbath."

"I went to the shul (synagogue) every Friday afternoon with my father," Lou tells his listeners. "We carried some wood to help for the fire in the stove there, to keep the place warm while the men prayed. The fire was lit by a non-Jew who worked there, of course, because we could not do this once the Sabbath started. Then we went home for the Sabbath meal. I walked with my father. I'm sorry to mention that my father was gassed at Auschwitz."

Before heading to the Synagogue, Priva would cover her eyes while blessing the Sabbath candles; and after dusk fell the Sabbath was welcomed and felt in the evening mist as Mordecai would chant the benedictions over the wine and the bread Priva had baked in the morning The candles would burn brightly against the Carpathian nightfall and the gathering darkness of history. The Dunst family felt somehow safe; a delicious, if tentative, peace would fill the simple structure that contained both a living home and a retail store.

Mordecai had served in the army of Austria-Hungary during World War I and had shivered and nearly starved as a POW in Siberia. His face was beaten with cold and worry and the constant wariness that came with life in a world of mostly antagonistic neighbors. Besides retaining skills as an electrician and a book binder, he was also a trained shopkeeper. He managed the incoming and outgoing flow of diverse goods, minding the inventory with exacting standards. Under his watchful eyes, stock came and went: ground corn meal, flour, grains, a variety of home supplies, and basic clothing needs, including pants, shirts, gloves, belts, and socks. "The gentiles bought a lot of shoes," says Lou. He also recalled that the store did a brisk business in an assortment of candies, "especially this good chocolate with nuts in it." From time to time, the gentile customers, short on coins, would trade for merchandise with fresh eggs.

In describing the store, the mucky streets, and the nearby mountains, Lou consistently returns to one of his central ethics: the family. "We were very close. We worked with each other, we shared everything, we helped and depended on one another. Among us, in the town, the Jewish people all knew each other and everything about each other. There was no craziness. There was no divorce. People worked out their problems. There was loyalty. People talked. We were good people. We were happy in our own circle. We were Jewish Orthodox and *shomer shabbas* (keeping and honoring the Sabbath). Our lives were all about giving and receiving and being charitable. There was none of this selfishness, this 'I'm doing my own thing' and not caring what the community needs. We looked after the poor and fed the hungry. We were good citizens, taxpayers. We were not criminals that should have gotten the treatment we got."

Like the other Jewish youngsters in Jasina, Lou attended a public school—often being attacked "by fascists" on the way to and from the lessons. "We tried to avoid them or get away from them by getting home before the sun went down." Eventually, with the advent of the infamous racially-tinged and virulently anti-Semitic Nuremberg Laws in 1935, the Jewish kids were barred from the community school. "We weren't bad boys or anything like that," says Lou. "We were thrown out because we were Jewish."

But, being Jewish, their education was supplemented by "*cheyder*" daily after regular school. The word literally means "room" and it is a familiar memory among older Jews of European descent. "*Cheyder*" was, in fact, a plain room—convened in a private home—with desks where the teachers, generally older students, and overseen by the local rabbi, drilled the younger in the Hebrew alphabet, the Jewish calendar, the weekly portion of Torah, and the commentaries of the rabbinic tradition, including Talmud and Mishnah.

Lou tells middle school children that he visits: "We were anxious to learn. We were very poor people but, yes, we were anxious to learn. The education is what we got from there. So, I say to you now: be good to your teachers. Be good to your parents. Because they are giving you something that is the most valuable thing you will ever get. You can't even lose it in Las Vegas; so be good to both of them, the teachers and the parents because they are very valuable."

The *cheyder* discussions were about ethics and wisdom and what the revered sages taught about life—everything from how and when to pray, how to share property, when to discipline a child, resolve conflicts, farm and reap while being sensitive to the earth's ecology, and how to be a proper husband or wife.

The pupils assembled all together; they were "from the ages of four to about eighteen," says Lou. "When there was a shortage of books, which there always was, we just shared the books. If we didn't have enough pencils, which we never did, we split the pencils into two or three pieces and shared them, too. We were just trying to learn our own ways. We would carry our own pieces of wood to the *cheyder* to keep the fire going because it was always cold. My mother made me a large package of food every day for lunch. I didn't understand at first—why so much? She would explain to me that the food wasn't only for me. It's for those other kids who didn't have what to eat. And she also explained to me that it wasn't so much about the food. It was about their feelings of shame that they were poor and hungry. That's what we did, we didn't know any other way. There we were, in the middle of nowhere, just trying to live good lives. Hitler still found us. I'm sorry to mention that my mother was gassed at Auschwitz."

But the Jewish children had normal desires and they knew that their way of life also cost them some of the fun and frolic that was due to children. "We Jewish kids didn't always love the fact that we had to go to *cheyder* after school," Lou explained. "It took away our time to enjoy the snow, like the other kids did. We missed out on the skiing that was a big thing then in that place, the skating, and all the games kids liked to make in the snow. But it was okay. We knew who we were."

With a great grin, Lou praises "a genius of a man," a scholarly tutor with whom he was paired with in *cheyder*, for filling Lou up with both the text and spirit of Jewish learning. His name was "*Zeyde*" Schnek. The name, "*Zeyde*" was an honorific (meaning "Grandpa"),given to someone special who had passed through illness or difficulty in life yet was still inspiring others. Schnek suffered from some deafness but his mind was sharp and his soul understanding. Lou exclaims, "He was a living computer!" He acclaims his long-ago teacher everywhere he goes, raising his arms above his rounded shoulders with pride and respect and gratitude. Because Lou, like all the other Jewish grade school kids, was banished from public school by the Nazis, and thus never received a formal education, he considers the hard-of-hearing teacher as being responsible for his very literacy.

The day after his eighty-seventh birthday, Lou stood before a largely non-Jewish audience at the Lions Club in downtown San Diego and practically shouted: "The man taught me everything and I'm still practicing everything he taught!" He repeated this avowal two days later in a ramshackle classroom of fifty juvenile delinquents who listened to his story in fascination and stillness.

Zeyde Schnek was gassed by the Nazis at Auschwitz.

Lou recalls the *"oberrabbiner,"* the chief rabbi, a man named Moshe Bergman. "He worked in the one synagogue that was in the center of the town. But there were several other synagogues here and there." The synagogues, for the most part feeble structures, were essentially the Jewish community centers. There the Yiddish-speaking townspeople would gather to pray, study pages of Talmud, discuss communal issues, seek counseling from the rabbi, and gauge the mood of the *goyim.*

Lou's life each day was a succession of Hebrew lessons, regular school, more Hebrew lessons, and then labor with his brother, sister, and parents in the store. Every day was like that; except for the Sabbath. "Everything stopped on Shabbat. It was beautiful."

Things didn't remain beautiful very long. In fact, with the dark and poisonous clouds of Nazism floating down the Carpathians and into every phase, aspect, liberty, and human characteristic that the Jews knew or coveted, Lou's Bar Mitzvah ceremony (the coming-of-age ritual normally experienced by boys at the age of 13) was moved up and performed early—when he was still a few months prior to being thirteen years old.

The men anxiously gathered at the synagogue, where Mordecai had years before laid a brick and made a donation to help set the building's foundation. The rabbi hurriedly had the boy bless and chant from the Torah scroll. Hitler had taken over Germany in 1933, the Nuremberg Laws that essentially separated the Jews from the Aryan civilization that despised and dehumanized them socially and legally shortly thereafter were already in effect. "The free world was out enjoying their martinis and not paying attention to what was starting to happen to us," bemoans Lou.

The Germans were both seizing land (including the "Sudetenland"—a section of Czechoslovakia with deep Germanic roots) and rousing the enthusiastically compliant Christian residents of this and many other regions to terrorize, round up, and murder Jews. Lou Dunst, an unimposing, kindly lad who loved his mother and father, had no idea how literally his improvised ceremony of "becoming a man" would be realized in the most horrifying and unimaginable ways.

LOU DUNST AT THE SPACE AND NAVAL WARFARE SYSTEMS COMMAND CENTER

LOU AT THE NAVY BASE SAN DIEGO

CHAPTER THREE

Three Torah Scrolls

A T THE UNITED STATES HOLOCAUST MUSEUM IN WASHINGTON, DC, there is an exhibit of an empty, hollow, long-ago re-stained and sanitized rail car. It is 31½ feet long and its interior space adds up a little more than 26 feet. The inner height of the car is 14 feet. The car is wooden, barren, and screams at you silently as you enter. You try very hard but are unable to even imagine what went on, who died and how many, and how the people who had been squeezed into it unmercifully and without any comprehension of their petrifying predicament and destiny must have felt while being piled within its dizzying confinement and its unbearable stench.

The Museum, which distills its unfathomable narration, archives, testimonies, and accounts into some kind of manageable public curriculum, offers this official account of the rail transport segments of the Nazi war against the Jews:

The Germans used both freight and passenger cars for the deportations. They did not provide the deportees with food or water, even when the transports had to wait days on railroad spurs for other trains to pass. The people deported in sealed freight cars suffered from intense heat in summer, freezing temperatures in winter, and the stench of urine and excrement. Aside from a bucket, there were no provisions for sanitary requirements. Without food or water, many deportees died before the trains reached their destinations. Armed guards shot anyone trying to escape. Between the fall of 1941 and the fall of 1944, millions of people were transported by rail to the extermination camps and other killing sites in occupied Poland and the occupied Soviet Union.

Lou Dunst, who, with his family, suffered through several of those interminable, darkly grotesque journeys in the notorious "box cars," states it simply—and from grim experience: "We were put together in there like sub-human beings. Not even sub-human. We had nothing but the clothes on our backs. They took all our luggage. They seized all of our belongings. The minute we were sealed in there, we didn't know where we were going, for how long, what day it was, if even it was day or night. There was one bucket in there for people to go to the bathroom. The conditions were unimaginable. When I'm telling you about it now, I cannot believe what I am remembering. Soon, the whole car was filled with urine and feces. It was a terrible smell and it never left your nostrils. Even now I can smell it in my memory. People couldn't breathe, we were gasping for a breath, fighting over one little hole in the wall where there was maybe a little breath of air. People were dying. Some were dead. Some gave birth. We had no idea where we were going and why and for how long."

[FROM THE UNITED STATES HOLOCAUST MUSEUM]

It's notable that whenever Lou speaks privately or publicly about any of the various frameworks or settings of his journey through hell, he always mentions, even as he describes the catalogue of horrors, that, yes, people were dying or already dead. Yet he invariably adds that "some were giving birth." On one hand, he is successfully conveying the complete lack of moral order in the gothic chaos of what the Germans did to the Jews. On the other hand, Lou seems unable not to make some reference to life even while carefully annotating the culture of death.

But for several years before the box cars, Lou and his family sensed that ghastly times were coming down the railroad. Wretched statutes passed by the Nazi-saturated German parliament, the notoriously racialist edicts known as the Nuremberg Laws, were passed enthusiastically in 1935. This is a standard reference point for Lou Dunst.

"Whenever there was something important going on in the community back at home in Jasina, every one of us would take part in it. We were human beings who saw great value in each other. We knew when this one was having a happy occasion, when that one was suffering a tragedy. We were decent people and we cared." Such are the recollections that Lou shares eight decades after his childhood, which unfolded with the Nazi takeover of Germany in 1933 and the subsequent "dehumanization" of the Jewish people that was ratified at Nuremberg.

"Here comes 1933," he recounts, "and Hitler came to power. And things started to go from bad to worse, from bad to worse. And soon comes 1935. The Nuremberg Laws were written. You can look it up, it's available in print. There were about 400 chapters. I will go into two or three of them."

ANNOUNCEMENT OF THE
NUREMBERG RACIAL LAWS

It was in Nuremberg, officially designated as the "City of the Reich Party Rallies," in the province of Bavaria, where Adolf Hitler and the Nazi Party in 1935 callously altered the legal status of German Jews. Now they were simply, helplessly, Jews in Germany, excluded, downgraded "subjects", thus formally instituting the context that eventually led to the Holocaust. It was now as permissible for a brown shirt thug in Jasina to beat up Lou Dunst as it was for officials throughout the Reich to outlaw marriage between the subhuman Jews and Aryans via these Laws.

The Law for the Protection of German Honor and German Blood not only proscribed marriages but also banned sexual intercourse between "Jews" and "Germans." It also prohibited the employment of "German" females under forty-five in Jewish households. The Reich Citizenship Law stripped Jews of their German nationality and introduced a new distinction between "Reich citizens" and "nationals." The term "Jews" was formally introduced as the new racial term for all non-Aryans.

Lou speaks to American teenagers who sit, mesmerized, in their classrooms about the Nuremberg Laws:

"One chapter deals with what they called 'Aryanization.' Jewish businesses were signed over to the Nazis. Everything that belonged to the Jews was taken away. And according to them, this was legal.

Other chapters dealt with '*Juden raus!*'—that the Jews had to 'get out,' that they couldn't use a swimming pool or bench in the park. Everywhere signs, 'Jews Not Allowed.' On the grocery stores, on the butcher shops, there were signs that 'Jews enter at their own risk.' In other words, if you walked in there, you could be attacked. Jewish doctors, dentists, lawyers, teachers were not allowed to practice.... Jewish children, including myself, I was about 11, were kicked out of school. Not because I was a bad boy! I'm Jewish!"

Lou wound up studying wood work—a tolerated vocation for a Jewish lad—in a "škola řezbářská," a trade school.

"They let us only do things with our hands for work. My brother and I both started with the wood. He stuck with it. I went later to different fields. I wound up at first working in the slaughterhouses."

The boys' youth and their relative dexterity worked in favor of their ultimate survival in a world where killing was quickly become rampant.

In 1938, a board game was unveiled in Nazi Germany and Austria that was wildly popular among Aryan families. It was called "*Juden raus!*" It was produced by a firm in Dresden called Günther & Co. The manufacturer-suggested user age was from 10 years and up. It employed dice that were spun and rolled across a board and was "recommended for six players."

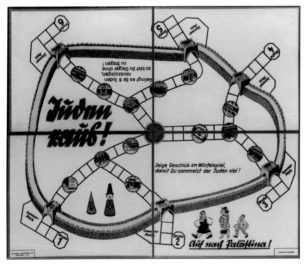

'JUDEN RAUS!' BOARD GAME

The family game depicts the policy of racial hatred that defined the Nazi era. It was made available just one month after *Kristallnacht* (The Night of the Broken Glass). This was the state-organized national pogrom of November 9–10, 1938. The *"Juden raus!"* family board game was designed by to simulate the torture of, and discrimination against, the Jewish people.

The board game was but one symptom of the era. Nazi propaganda—one of the most sinisterly effective campaigns in world history—extended to every form of media: there were postage stamps marked with the phrase *"Judenfrei"* ["free of Jews"], short-subject movies, cartoons, billboards, books, and radio commercials. Another term frequently applied was *"Judenrein"*—meaning that a building, a store, a neighborhood, a city, or an entire region was literally "clean of Jews." This had the even more ominous implication that any trace of Jewish blood had been eliminated as an infection or toxin. While Lou Dunst was just coming into adolescence, when he and his siblings and friends should have been free to explore life and experience the natural transition to adulthood, they were all being treated and/or eliminated as "contaminants."

German and Austrian schoolchildren were taught to recite odes and poems in their schools, including this one:

> *Keep your blood pure,*
> *It is not yours alone,*
> *It comes from far away,*
> *It flows into the distance*
> *Laden with thousands of ancestors,*
> *And it holds the entire future!*
> *It is your eternal life.*

From Gelnhausen, Germany to Bydgoszcz, Poland to Vienna, Austria and on through Luxemburg, Estonia, Serbia, Czechoslovakia, Russia, France, Denmark, and beyond, Nazi newspapers reported synagogues closed and towns "cleansed" and Jews eliminated and the place redeemed as *"Judenrein"*—even as little kids rolled the dice with their parents on a board game that was but a household replication of a continental massacre. His voice dropping from its normal informational calm, Lou describes how the Nazis or their local collaborators would come into towns like his own, round up the Jews and seal them into the area synagogue, then throw grenades and torches into the building so that they would burn alive inside. "They had to fulfill what they called the elimination of *Rassenschande*, (Race Disgrace)," he sadly recounts.

"They took away our homes and moved into them. They took our clothing, our valuables, our property, and when we were dead or sometimes even if we were not dead yet, they took our gold fillings. Gold they took from us like crazy, even if we were hiding it inside our bodies. This was a typical practice. They warned us to turn over anything we were hiding. I don't mean hiding in our pockets. We were naked; we didn't even have our clothes. If we didn't give up the gold or jewels we were hiding in our body cavities, they would get them in the most painful ways. You can't imagine. I learned how to hide things in the scrotum. They found things on people, in people in places and in ways that you cannot even imagine."

It has been reported in many sources that Nazi or Nazi-crazed men habitually violated their very own "race disgrace" laws by routinely raping Jewish women and girls, then cutting off their breasts and relieving them of any personal valuables they had tried to hide—in even the most intimate places. The bodies of the disposed females were then summarily dumped into heaps to be burned or just to rot in the sun.

Europe was convulsing with Nazi brutality and with the most sinister and mind-bending inhumanity ever known in history. The list of atrocities will never be finalized. On December 16, 1939, Jewish girls in Lodz, Poland were already working for weeks and weeks in forced labor. On impulse from their crazed taskmasters, they were dragged out of the routine and forced to scrub latrines with their own blouses. When the toilets were considered clean, the Germans wrapped the soiled blouses around the girls' faces.

....

"Our blood was contaminated, according to them, and their blood was 100% pure." This is the phrase Lou Dunst uses to succinctly describe the Nazi racial doctrines that robbed him of both his childhood and his parents. Then, with a trace of resentful glee, he declares: "Of course it was a lie! Because when they needed blood for their wounded soldiers on the Russian front, they took our blood for their soldiers." Lou generally spares his audiences the details of how the Nazis and their accomplices actually extracted the blood from Jewish adults and children to help save the lives of their soldiers besieged in Stalingrad or holed up in France or shot down over Poland.

"Here comes 1938—*Anschluss*. The Nazis marched into Austria. They were greeted with open arms, flowers, kisses. There were plenty of Nazis at that time in Austria. So they didn't waste too much time, they picked up Jewish people, beat them in the streets, invading their homes, making them to clean streets and toilets with hand brushes and toothbrushes, spitting at them, kicking them, urinating on their heads to dehumanize them, to demoralize them. They would cut off the beards of the Jewish men right in public, laughing and punching them. Many people were taken to concentration camps for a one-way trip."

The term *"Anschluss"* means "union" in German. Adolf Hitler, after a series of bullying and threatening gestures, nonetheless met little resistance to his declaration of a formal merger of Germany and Austria on March 12, 1938. In some ways, this was redundant—such a union had been a dream of Austrian fascists for decades and Hitler was a native of Austria. A phony "plebiscite" of Austria's citizens asking for approval of the union was ratified by 99.7%. The Fuhrer again had his terrifying way and the Jews of Austria now found themselves lethally exposed in a nation that no longer existed but as an enlargement of the Third Reich. Lou Dunst, in his simple, disarming manner makes it clear: the irony was that the cheering Austrians were now part of a nameless entity even as the Jews they despised were a nameless people.

"Jewish artifacts were destroyed," relates Lou. "Jewish books were thrown into big fires. Synagogues were burning. After *Kristallnacht*, Hitler made a big speech and a lot of people came to hear him speak. A lot of people. He spoke and everybody was screaming '*Heil Hitler! Heil Hitler!* You're doing a good job, go and get them!' By 'them' he meant the Jews."

Indeed, the sanctioned removal of Jewish families from their homes, many of which they lived in for generations, began and cascaded. As it was in Berlin, now it was in Vienna: all Jewish professional licenses, academic degrees, and citizenship rights were annulled forever. Jewish children were expelled from schools. Fathers and brothers were hauled away in frightful nighttime raids that began with Gestapo agents or their deputies banging on the doors of sleeping Jewish families. *"Juden! Raus!"* ("Jews! Out!") Most of the men were never seen again. "They moved into our homes, took out furniture, our bank accounts, and our lives," says Lou. "Not one person said, 'Wait a minute! What are we doing to our neighbors?' No one said anything against what was being done to us."

It happened at the Dunst home in Jasina as well. The local Ukrainians had been given the order by the Nazis that all the Jews were to be liquidated. An initial step in this project was, in Lou's terms, "to develop a list of all the Jewish men to be hanged. My father was on that list. It did not transpire." Somehow,

Mordecai escaped that fate but now the local thugs were preparing to simply take him away. A list was posted and again the name of Mordecai Dunst was on it. On a given time and at a stated hour, he was to "report." Where he'd be going and what he'd be doing were only matters of horrendous speculation. Again and again, Lou has said: "We did not have time to think. I don't know how to describe the whole thing. Because it was such a fear and such a depression. We could not even function. Our brains would not work normally."

Lou had nightmares then and he experiences nightmares to this day.

In one such dream, the pounding on the door shakes the building that combined the Dunst home and store. There is pale moonlight outside as Lou and Irving awaken, staring at each other in horror and anguish. Their mother and sister rush past in the hallway; the boys think they hear muffled screams audible even above the hollering at the doorway and the blunt thumping and the blood-curdling shouts: "Raus! *Juden, raus!*" Before the boys can even comprehend what is happening, they hear boots clamping down hard on the floor below and cruel-sounding, power-drunk men are demanding their father: "Mordecai Dunst! *Schnell!*"

Priva, her hands trembling beyond control, lights a lamp in the entranceway, managing to do it even while holding onto her little girl, Risi. The boys have crept into a shadowy edge of the main room. Mordecai appears, his eyes hollow, clearly frightened, but resigned to what is happening. Lou awakens from this terror in 1940. He awakens from this terror in 2013.

Jewish men were being taken from their homes at a regular clip in such brutish nocturnal raids—ostensibly to work in labor camps, if not to be quickly killed. The apprehenders were often not German soldiers. They were the Ukrainians or Czechs or Hungarians who did their work with evil amusement and were paid for every Jew with a couple of coins and a pinch of rum.

The stunned Jewish relatives would blink into the morning sun a few hours later and murmur things to one another and among other families: "It could be worse. He could have been killed. He will come back after this madness passes."

But Lou had stared out the window for a long time after his father left "to report." For the increasingly blood-lusting community of Europe, Mordecai Dunst was just another statistical possibility, a unit, an inhuman creature good only for work and disposal—another digital redemption of the insipid, malignant, unbound anti-Semitism that now, after centuries of percolating, was boiling over in cosmic, apocalyptic terms. But to Lou, his father, Mordecai, son of Daniel, was the somewhat stern but warm-hearted, cautious, dignified man. He was center of the universe that suddenly had no center, no bearings, no arc, and no hope.

Holding back tears as best he could, Lou thought of his father's heavy, tie-up shoes, always muddy from the dismal streets of Jasina or dusty from the busy floor of the store. He thought about the time that a young fascist brute attacked Mordecai in the village. The attacker came close to choking Mordecai to death. Brother Irving came running with a brick with which he struck the bully and thus saved his father's life.

Now Lou wondered gloomily how it would be to wash his own shoes in the river on the coming Friday afternoon in preparation for the Sabbath. His father's presence, the soft words that Mordecai spoke, giving direction, encouragement, and liturgical structure—the sudden absence of these made Lou feel orphaned, disconnected, and profoundly scared. Yet even with this glaring invasion of the family normalcy, the thought of not washing the mud off his shoes on Friday, of not having the Sabbath, with its candles, wine, and challah—these things never occurred to the boy. "The unity of the family is above everything," Lou repeats and repeats to everyone who will listen in a new century and at a time when there are few families that were ever like the Dunst household.

Nearly eighty years later, Lou recalls his father with clarity and love.

First he puts his father on the map. The Nazis may have tried to obliterate his childhood home, and they did succeed in blurring or erasing counties, regions, and even nations. But they could not erase memory and faces and Hebrew words and priceless ideas that fathers taught their sons.

"In school," recalls Lou, "we learned about Czechoslovakia. And we followed that map. This is Sudetenland, this is Bohemia, this is Moravia, this is Slovakia, this is the Carpathian Mountains. The capital city of Prague is over here and we, my family, we lived over here." He draws along his imaginary map, indicating the more industrial complexes near Prague and the manufacturing centers of Moravia. "Then comes Slovakia—there was more agriculture. Then we come to my area in the mountains, and there was really only one area of production and that was wood: forests. We had mills. Most of the mills were owned by Jews. They would bring in the lumber and cut it up inside the sawmills and they made boards. They shipped the boards out all over the country, even to the world. That was the biggest thing that kept things alive for us and that was the lumber. All from my town of Jasina."

Lou points to the desk in front of him, conjuring up the memory of a place that once made sense, a place of steaming soup and warm bread and Torah scrolls and Sabbath prayers. He even smiles while recalling "the apples that were as small as plums, the little potatoes and tiny pears because it was so cold all the time and the soil wasn't so good." The earth in that region was pale and stubborn and there was but a smattering of trees and a cluster of tough wells. Lou's fingers emphatically thump upon remembered coordinates of a time and a life that was swept away. His father's face and eyes and strong back are hanging somewhere between his work worn hands; his mouth is curled in grief and conviction.

"My father was a little more educated than some of the people in the town. Not so much more, but a little bit. He was trained as an electrician. He had this skill. But he was also a bookbinder. He was just knowledgeable in many fields. He was a businessman. He studied to become a retailer. In Europe, you had to do that. He was the president of the little *shul* that we went to. He kept track of the donations; they weren't such big donations, people were poor but still they gave. He was the one who kept a list of the various projects the *shul* did, of getting some food to the hungry people, of making sure that the sick were visited. He saw about the money in the *shul*, what went in from there and what went out to there. And he was respected for this, and other things he did."

Was he a loving father? Lou was asked.

"Yes. Well, you know, he had a bicycle. It was like having a Rolls Royce today! Maybe only one in a hundred families had a bicycle. He would take us sometimes to school or to the *cheyder* on his bicycle. In other words, he was a good father. In those days, it was different how the families were structured. Nobody was bad, they were all good people, they were all good neighbors, and they were all good business associates. They were all loving parents." Lou curled his hands, suggesting a kind of natural intimacy in the town, and said: "Because it was a very small community with a unity where everybody knew everybody. There was no 'strict Orthodox,' just 'Orthodox.' Everybody was '*shomer shabbas*' ('keeper of the Sabbath') and kosher. There were no divorces. People usually just married people they already knew. My father, like everybody else, had to buy things in order to sell them in the store. So he had to communicate with all kinds of people. Like the flour—he would talk with the one who sold that. And then the clothing, he would talk to this one over here. That's how it was. He was good at everything he did."

It seems as though, when Lou is asked if his father was a loving parent, that the phrase has always been redundant for him.

During Mordecai's absence, Lou would turn for some comfort and company (aside from his brother, sister, and mother) to one friend he had in the town, Shlomo Moskovitz. There wasn't that much to do in terms of play and recreation and the segregated Jewish boys were also burdened with work and studies. "But Shlomo and I would sort of get together, usually on the Sabbath, and take a little walk into the center of the town. We would do this and that. There was no work on Saturday. Sometimes we'd go and study with some of the others, maybe the *Pirkei Avot* ('The Chapters of the Fathers' section of Talmud). Sometimes, we'd just go around to see and be seen." The memories of the Jewish children in those troubled times, like the actual experiences they shared together, are scant and fleeting.

The abduction of men and older boys from their homes—an initial phase of the developing "Final Solution of the Jewish People"—was, in the case of the Dunst family, a direct result of the issue of the Sudetenland. "Hitler decided he needed more space for the German people," Lou recounts for his audience.

Sudetenland was a Czech region that had always been ethnically German. Hitler saw an opportunity to expand the Nazi expanse and played upon the Sudeten Germans' fiery nationalism. Following the *Anschluss*, Hitler was eyeing his objective of *Grossdeutschland*—a Greater Germany extending from Austria to Czechoslovakia. Incorporating Sudetenland into Germany would go a long way towards fulfilling this aim.

In May, 1938, when Lou Dunst was 12, Hitler ordered German troops into positions along the border with Sudetenland. Hitler cynically assured the international community that he just wanted was the ethnic Germans to get what they wanted and join Germany. None of this was good for the Jews, of course. The Munich Agreement, brokered with the shameful appeasement of Britain's Prime Minister Neville Chamberlain, ceded Sudetenland to the Nazis and further sealed the fate of the Dunst family and every Jewish child, woman, and man in Czechoslovakia.

"So it was 1940 and my father was rounded up for the slave labor," mourns Lou. "They used Jewish men often to be their minesweepers. They did not regard us as being people. So they threw the Jewish men where they thought there might be mines and of course all of us who were used for that purpose were killed. Eventually, my brother Irving and I, because we were strong teenagers were also doing slave labor, loading their armaments and all the kinds of the things slaves could do."

Lou carries vivid memories of a regal, stately Nazi officer named Friedrich Wilhelm Krüger—"Hauptman" (Captain) Krüger, which means "chief." The process of "Aryanization" was underway; Lou says, "it was already cooking, the whole thing." Anti-Semites appointed by the Nazis were already appropriating Jewish establishments; "there was a Nazi, or someone put there by the Nazis, that was in my father's store. They took away the retail certificate to sell. In other words, my father did not any longer have a selling license."

With glistening boots, immaculate fingernails, coiffed hair, imperial belts, and shiny medals, all adorning a shimmering black uniform topped off with the swastika, Hauptman Friedrich-Wilhelm Krüger marched about Jasina and its environs like a bureaucratic cavalier. His bureaucracy: the Jews. Says Lou about the imposing constable: "He introduced himself as 'Hauptman Krüger, Policajscheff'—he was the top of the police, the highest rank that the police could have. When we asked him once, what was his responsibility, he simply said, 'I am in the charge of the Jews in this area.' He did not mention any killing or torturing or anything like that. I am sure he did not go out into the field himself and do these things. He had thousands of people working for him. "

Lou describes the captain as always being refined and polite. "He never used bad language and never asked for anything and expected to pay nothing for it. My brother and I would try and figure out why he would come into our house and store, always so polite and so nice. I even remember that one day he took off his gold ring and put it on the scale. We could never understand why he did that."

Lou and Irving from time to time discussed, both during and after the war, why Krüger was so courteous to the Dunst family (given the fact that he commanded countless squads of *Einsatzngruppen* killing units that machine-gun-massacred Jews). "We figured out," says Lou, "that since the war was going the wrong way for the Germans after Stalingrad, he wanted to get some nice recommendations from us later at any trials that might come up."

Hauptman Krüger would occasionally materialize at the Dunst home on Friday evenings, replete with his normal small entourage of soldiers, just to wish the family a cheery "Good Shabbos!" He would walk into the family store from time to time and ask Mordecai for the delivery of some particular Hungarian salami that he craved. At one time, Lou's mother Priva even thought to entreat the mannerly police captain to help in the delivery of some relatives from the town just across the nearby border that was also under Krüger's jurisdiction. She never got up the nerve.

In fact, SS Captain Friedrich-Wilhelm Krüger was responsible for the mass-murder operations carried out by the Border Police and the SS. He received orders directly from Heinrich Himmler, one of Hitler's top lieutenants and the man who personally managed the "Final Solution of the Jewish Question." Krüger was present at the heinous Wannsee Conference of January 1942, where, over coffee and cake, the most senior Nazis signed off the pact that sealed the genocide of six million Jews.

Krüger's administrative region was large and extensive. He operated primarily from a secret police station but traveled widely and in style. According to the Shoah Resource Center of the Yad Vashem Holocaust Memorial in Jerusalem:

> Over the span of sixteen months, this small police station—its staff at times numbering only twenty-five—organized and implemented the shooting of some 70,000 Jews and the deportation of another 12,000 to death camps. Acts of such monstrous proportions are generally associated only with the large SS killing squads that operated in the occupied Soviet Union.

Krüger followed the examples of his mentors, including Himmler and Hitler, committing suicide in 1945.

LEFT: SS HAUPTMAN FRIEDRICH-WILHELM KRÜGER.
RIGHT: ABANDONED CORPSES BEING REMOVED FROM THE EBENSEE CAMP STREETS.

When Mordecai Dunst inexplicably returned from the labor camp, Lou and his family certainly breathed sighs of relief. But there was no outburst of emotion, no visible celebration. The situation had already robbed the family of its ability to feel and experience and certainly to rejoice about anything. The father stepped back into the rotation of existence almost as mechanically as he had left in submission to "the list." It was just a question of making it through another day, holding on to some food, trying to make any sense of what was happening, and coexisting with the permanent numb of foreboding that had replaced any vestige of a normal life.

Before long, the decree came: all the Jews of Jasina were to gather for relocation. Amid murmurs of "It could be worse..." and some dogged refrains of "Hitler won't last..." and a seething fear that both possibilities were dark fantasies, the children and adults of the town, some with Hebrew prayers on their lips, prepared for the next drop into the abyss. Suitcases were hastily and nervously packed, mezuzahs removed from doorways or simply kissed with a tear, and precious items, such as gold pieces and jewelry, hidden. And that often meant secreted by swallowing or depositing into any possible notch on or in the human body.

Mordecai and Priva had a desperate idea: send little Lu-Lu into hiding, somehow. He tells the story:

> When we were taken away from our homes, this is what happened:— we were just taken away from our homes. We had three cows. This is what we had: cows, milk, some chickens. We were just a little bit above the others financially. So my parents told me to take one cow and go to a Christian man we knew. He had a retail store, also. By the name of Vizaver. They told me, my parents, you give him the cow, and he will hide you. It's a good deal for him to hide you away. This is exactly what happened. What parents say, that goes! I took one of the cows and went to this non-Jew, Christian, and told him the story that I'll give him the cow if he will hide me out. We were figuring that it was going to be for a day or two or three and that's all. No one was imagining such a thing as was going to happen.
>
> So he listened to me and he agreed. And the place to hide me, most of those houses are built that in the room there is a small hole. Not so much room that a human being could go in there and hide out. Like what we used it in the summertime to keep things cool and in the wintertime to keep things from freezing. So I got in there, there was not enough space for me to stand up. And right away, things go through my mind. Like a million things in a second. What went through my mind, just to describe it a little bit, what is the best thing and the worst thing that can happen here? There

were cases where people that hid Jewish people, they just killed them off. They didn't want to be responsible. After all, if they were caught, they would be punished. *Boom-boom.* That's all.

So I don't know if this Christian is going to just kill me off and not take a chance. And have a cow. So the last thought that went through my mind was, what if I was saved, he didn't kill me but all my people would not be alive, what would be my life? So I went out. And I went back to my family.

Lou relates, when questioned, why did his parents plan to hide him but not his brother and sister, Irving and Risi? "Well, look, everybody had different circumstances. It just so happened that I was on good terms with this Vizaver." Decades later, Lou returned during one of his many visits to Jasina and the area. "I found his daughters, this Vizaver. He died but I found his two daughters. When I told them who I was and what happened, they cried and cried."

But Lou noted the tears with tenderness, without skepticism. "It just couldn't be known what he, Vizaver, was really thinking about at the time. Maybe he would get tired of feeding me. Maybe he would just be worried about being punished for hiding some Jew and then he just kills me off. And he still has the cow. Who knows? There were too many details, too many branches in the tree."

All five of members of the Dunst family were taken, with every last Jew in Jasina, to a large theater in the center of the town, the "Corona." They were processed, pushed, spat upon, kicked, and worse. They were then told to re-gather in the cemetery at the edge of the town within a short time in order to prepare for "relocation."

Mordecai took Lou by the hand. As quickly and discreetly as possible, the two of them slipped off to the little synagogue—where years before Mordecai put down a brick and a donation to help fund the House of God. The boy and his father carried off the three Torah Scrolls and rushed back to their home with the holy objects. With delicate hands and wet eyes, they set the scrolls down in a clean corner of the house, straightened the crowns and breastplates, adjusted the silver pointers, and smoothed the mantles. Wordlessly, they bowed and kissed all three of the sheepskin scrolls.

"That was the last time I ever saw those scrolls," says Lou, with sadness. "Nobody knows what happened to them."

Then they reported to the cemetery.

LOU DUNST'S MOTHER AND FATHER

THE THREE DUNST CHILDREN,
IRVING, RISI, AND LOU; JASINA, 1932

CHAPTER FOUR

A Trail of Suffering

I N THE *NEW UNION PRAYER BOOK* OF THE CENTRAL CONFERENCE OF American Rabbis, there is a reading that precedes the Mourner's Kaddish and specifically deals with the recollection of "Our Martyrs." It references horrific places where Jews were shot or gassed in massive numbers, including Dachau, Buchenwald, and Babi Yar (a ravine near Kiev where a number of machine gun massacres took place, including the most notorious single operation: the extermination of 33,771 Jews on September 29–30, 1941).

> What can we say? What can we do? How bear the unbearable, or accept what life has brought to our people? All who are born must die, but how shall we compare the slow passage of our time with the callous slaughter of the innocent, cut off before their time?

The prayer then continues with an assertion that is perhaps questionable for some:

> They lived with faith. Not all, but many. And, surely, many died with faith; faith in God, in life, in the goodness that even flames cannot destroy.

In fact, we don't know how many among the six million Jews who were vaporized by the Germans and their accomplices were people of religious faith or devotees of the liturgy or kept kosher or even believed in God before the expulsions, the tortures, the ghettoization, the medical experiments, the mass executions, and the gassings were underway. We have heard conflicting reports from survivors and/or their children (a generation afflicted with a unique and wretched clinical pain and guilt) about the victims and their faith. Some felt totally abandoned by God—to the point where they would have given anything to have hidden their Jewish religious backgrounds in order to possibly escape the fate that awaited them. Some bitterly proclaimed that this unfathomable development completely disproved the existence of God and any possible reason to even be Jewish. Others, however, would have found the entire horror unendurable but for their faith in God; God was the only reliable source of hope and the one place in their minds wherein there was some release from the terrifying reality and the profound loneliness and sense of abandonment—not to mention the scorching hunger, pain, and despair.

Lou Dunst might have been lost to us were it not for his unshakeable faith in God, whom he calls "*Ha-Shem.*" Even the use of this term, which means "The Name," reveals Lou's deep and mystic relationship with the God whom many felt abandoned the Jews in that darkest hour of their history.

Over and over again, to the enraptured audiences he addresses around the world, the roundish man with the sweet smile declares: "Never did I lose my faith in *Ha-Shem. Never.*" Lou is not hesitant to describe in great detail, the various atrocities committed by the Nazis and their eager partners in Ukraine, Hungary, France, and elsewhere. Although his voice rarely rises, his intermittent anger and incredulity at what he and his loved ones suffered is clearly apparent in occasional high-pitched bursts.

Standing there in front of high school pupils or executives, unadorned but for his yarmulke atop his head, usually in blue jeans and a simple shirt, he is at once accessible and spellbinding. To a new generation of children numb to violence as a result of the cyber-culture and the uncensored 24-hour news cycle, he is a hypnotic presence who simply uses words, memories, and ideas. It's almost as if these youngsters, temporarily disconnected from their cellular phones and broken off from their endless, digital stream of text messaging, were hungry for such a compelling, haunting story conveyed without graphics, music, or any computerized, artificial embellishments.

Living in a world of religious skepticism and spiritual ambivalence, these young people are disarmed by an old man with a funny accent and a strange syntax just telling them what happened and how God helped him through the most ungodly circumstances.

Lou tells his audiences straightforwardly, without fanfare, "They turned our ashes into fertilizer, they made soup from our flesh, and they converted our hair into all kinds of household products. They also made gloves from our skin. I saw this; I saw the gloves they made from us, in a museum in Ukraine."

One asks: how does a man who lived through hell stand up to praise heaven? Perhaps he keeps his mind healthy and his heart "clean," as he often says, by focusing on the details. He remembers what Dr. Josef Mengele, "The Butcher of Auschwitz," looked and sounded like. He matter-of-factly discusses Mengele's unutterable medical experiments on Jewish twins, allowing the basic description of these unimaginable deeds to speak plainly in their grisliness. In that ultimate death camp, Auschwitz, Lou recalls that two cousins of his—who happened to be twins—were taken away by Mengele for his depraved and gruesome research. Twins were given a modicum of special treatment, including candy and chocolates, and they were often allowed to keep their own clothing, and usually were not shaven clean like most inmates. These *"Zwillinge"* (twins) were scoped out by the Nazi guards at the Auschwitz rail depot, seized and separated from their screaming parents, tattooed, and then systematically put through horrifying procedures to help the Nazis learn "the secrets of heredity."

They were operated on, had their organs removed, their hearts pinched with needles, blood drawn from their necks, their brains manipulated with prongs, their eyes blinded—all in the interest of Aryan medical and biological planning. None of this was done with anesthetization. "Mengele's Children" suffered in a category that remains unrivaled in human annals.

Lou says about his twin cousins: "They survived, but they went crazy from what was done to them. They died soon after everything was over."

He recalls the many summations spoken to him and the other inmates, barked or screamed by Nazi officers of various rank and cruelty, "reassuring" them that there was no need for food—they were all going to be gassed, anyway.

But the same propensity for memory, which channels a purpose through his head as well as the narrative, also keeps alive more pleasant memories. Lou describes a running résumé of his father's many talents: retailer, bookkeeper, electrician, community organizer. Lou's uncle Abraham, was a trained and skilled kosher butcher who taught him the trade: "He would show me how to properly and humanely slaughter a cow. He would surgically make a distinction between the veins that contained the white blood cells and the red blood cells. I learned to do this distinction myself, the right way."

When you have witnessed, endured, and survived the greatest human slaughter of all time, and you have seen the value of human life reduced to filth, why wouldn't you revere the memory of your family's koshering of animals in favor of both feeding the hungry and honoring the tradition laid down by Scripture?

....

"We were living somewhere in the middle of the world, nowhere really, and somehow Hitler found us," Lou likes to say. People will occasionally giggle quietly at the remark—more a nervous reaction to the bitter humor than a chortle. They become very quiet, deeply affected when he repeats his adulation of "the unity of the family, the closeness, the reliability…the love of a family is stronger than death."

"We learned in the *cheyder* that we have to do the good deeds written in the Torah. Well, there's not many, only 613 [again the nervous chuckles] so we learned them and did them and I live by them to this day."

By 1939, the war was underway. Germany invaded Poland on September 1 and, as Lou tells it, "the Poles gave up in less than a month." This was the "Blitzkrieg"—the "lightning war." In fact, the Germans, who had been humiliated by the terms of the 1919 Versailles Treaty that concluded the First World War, had amassed the greatest concentration and arsenal of armaments and airpower in the history of the world to that point. It was also the first fully motorized saturation operation in military annals. Overrunning Europe quickly and brutally and efficiently was the objective; finding and killing every single Jew was the linked obsession. Some Nazi tanks were even emblazoned with the declaration "We are coming to Poland to eliminate the Jews!"

Of the six million Jewish victims of this genocide, three million were Polish.

"The Germans had given our section of Czechoslovakia [ceded in 1938] to the Ukrainians. They in turn wound up giving it to the Hungarians. They were all Nazis and they immediately began making things go from bad to worse."

Before long, the *Einsatzgruppen* killing squads were operating in and around "Zone D" of Czechoslovakia (under the grim administration of Hauptman Krüger), which included Jasina, and the Dunst children were hearing about and witnessing massacres and the subsequent looting of bodies.

"They came and took groups of us. They took people and lined them up and then made them dig their own graves. They made them to take off their clothes, their shoes, everything. They were completely naked. They machine-gunned them, men, women, and children. As long as someone was moving, there goes the machine-gun. *Dat-dat-dat-dat-dat.* Some were buried while they were still alive. Some were able to crawl out of those mass graves. They took their gold teeth, their fillings, their clothes, their belongings — everything. By that time they had run out of ammunition, bullets, so they tied their wrists and ankles and threw them into the river so that they would drown." Lou pauses when he communicates this. He clearly still cannot believe what he is relaying from his own memories.

"One night, there is a knock on the door. A young lady is standing there, maybe seventeen years old. She was one of those that survived out of that river, with her hands and feet tied up. How she did it, this is another miracle. A miracle of miracles. So we gave her a change of clothes and helped her clean up. We gave her some money to go and look for her parents or relatives. Hopefully, she had people, so that she and her family survived. We have not ever heard from her or anybody from her family. Later we found out that maybe one of the reasons that she survived that river was that she was a swimming champion."

Lou pauses, as though to offer a prayer: "I repeat her name. Charlotte Schartzwaltd."

Then, just a few days after the mysterious swimmer left the Dunst house, there was another knock on the door—this one much harder and belligerent. "They came in. Everybody has to get ready to go out. They told us that this was martial law and if you don't obey us and do what we tell you to do immediately, then we will take the pistol and shoot you."

Then Lou adds, "If somebody is sick in the bed and he can't get out, shoot him! Shooting Jewish people was like a game."

"The Jews were chased into the downtown section of the village. We were pushed and shoved and thrown into the largest building in the town—a theater called "Corona."

"We didn't all fit in there so some of us had to stay outside in the mud and the dirt, in the cold and the rain and so on. Several days later, we were marched to the Jewish cemetery at the edge of our little town. We were lined up there and some of the secrets were leaked that we would have to dig our own graves and that we would be gunned down. All we could do was to sit down and pray to our God, to *Ha-Shem*. And that's exactly what we did. Everybody prayed in his own way, the best he could."

Lou explains that most of the Jewish people in his part of the world actually were not transported to Auschwitz. Most of them were simply gunned down or burned to death in the synagogues of their small towns. "When there were no more Jews left, say in Estonia, they would call Hitler and notify him that the region was now '*Judenfrei*'—free of Jews."

SYNAGOGUE IN GERMAN-
OCCUPIED BYDGOSZCZ.
THE INSCRIPTION READS,
"THIS CITY IS FREE OF JEWS"

This cycle, this dynamic, this incomprehensible reality, remains the central memory of Lou Dunst's adolescence. It was happening everywhere, he says, in Galicia, White Russia, Lithuania, Latvia, Ukraine, and many regions beyond.

The Jews of Jasina were in this ghastly limbo, while being denied sustenance, being humiliated, beaten, randomly shot, or raped, for several days. It was during the 1940's and this scene was being repeated in several thousand other towns and villages and open fields across Europe. In Lodz, Poland, the Nazis had already forbidden Jews from traveling on trains and had sealed most of them in a new ghetto. There had been a massive execution of Poles perpetrated by the Germans in the city of Poznań, Warthegau.

"And the same incomprehensible cycle thing was waiting for us. They were there, just in front of us, with their machine guns, their shovels, their uniforms, their trucks, ready to do a good day's work. They even brought in civilian people from the town to help them do a good job. They were all ready to do it, to kill us. But then something happened. They either got a telegram or whatever. Something different happened and we were rounded up and taken to the railroad. Into boxcars. Jam-packed. A hundred in each one, as many as they could push in with force. Without food, without water, without toilet facilities. Not enough air to breathe. Doors locked from the outside. Off we go, stop and go. The reason the stop and go was to hook up other boxcars and other trains from wherever they could, from other cities and other towns and maybe even other countries."

Lou explains that none of them knew what country they were in at any time, or what time it even was, or how they had not even a shred of an idea of where they were going or why. Finally, the horror ride came to end: "We were in a small city by the name of Mátészalka in Hungary. We were put into a GHETTO. [Lou emphasizes such words.] We were fenced in like animals. Small space, lot of people without water, without food. And we were told, you step over here, you get shot. Pregnant women would get shot. And there was this assassin over here, a tall one, with his machine gun. And he had a long stick with nails sticking out of the other end and he just hit anybody over the head when he could reach. Without saying or asking anything. That was his job to do."

A German U-Boot torpedoed the Dutch trade ship *Arendskerk*. *Reichsführer-SS* Heimlich Himmler ordered the formal construction of the Auschwitz concentration and extermination camp—where the Dunst family would eventually be headed.

The western world more or less went about its business. In the United States, the Federal Communications Commission successfully completed its first transmission of FM radio with a clear, static-free signal. Frank Sinatra made his professional singing debut in Indianapolis with the Tommy Dorsey Orchestra. Walt Disney premiered his second feature-length movie, *Pinocchio*, in New York City. *Gone With the Wind* captured eight Oscars, including "Best Picture" (beating out *The Wizard of Oz*) at the Academy Awards in Hollywood. The New York Rangers won the 1940 Stanley Cup Finals in professional ice hockey.

Meanwhile, the Nazis were pummeling Poland, invading France, Norway, Czechoslovakia, and Russia, while obsessively killing Jews in every direction. In Hungary, where Lou and his family were suddenly transported by boxcar to the Mátészalka ghetto, the Hungarian people were enthusiastically joining in the anti-Semitic activities. The Dohány Street Synagogue of Budapest, one of the most time-honored and physically imposing synagogues in the world, a Moorish-style edifice that served as the border of Budapest's own Jewish ghetto, was vandalized and desecrated. The Hungarians converted the towering sanctuary into a stable for horses and cattle.

Mordecai, Priva, Risi, Irving, and Lou Dunst were dumped out of the boxcar at the ghetto. As bad it was, it was for but an interim of a month or so, until further train transports could be organized to take the Jews to their deaths in places like Auschwitz. In the Mátészalka ghetto, the Jews were forced to do menial, mean-ingless, and dehumanizing work: a favorite practice of the Nazis was to require the Jews to sweep stones and rocks across the street and back the other way—for hours and days without cease. The photo below captures this unique cruelty:

The town of Mátészalka is in the Satmar District. In Mátészalka itself, there lived 1,555 Jews among a total population of 10,036. The sealed ghetto in which the Dunsts were incarcerated was one of the bigger concentrations of Jews before their deportation for annihilation at Auschwitz. Ultimately, about 17,000 Jews were cramped and tortured in this confined quarter.

A small fraction of this prison population came from the town itself and several surrounding communities. Most prisoners, like the Dunsts of Jasina, all totaling 15,000, were conveyed from more than thirty localities in the Marmaros region. A Holocaust history publication has declared that "the conditions of this ghetto were shocking, and among the worst—of all the ghettos in Hungary." The report continues:

> At first, the Jews were concentrated outdoors. After some time, they were transferred to small shanties, most of them temporary. The Marmaros Jews suffered doubly here. For in addition to the usual suffering of all the inmates of the ghetto, the Jews of Marmaros also suffered because they were torn from their natural environment and were brought to foreign surroundings.

"Living conditions" in the ghettos such as Mátészalka were appalling and abysmal. It was typical for teenagers like Lou—and much younger children—to see abandoned corpses, their lifeless eyes open, the mouths agape with suffering, strewn about the streets, attracting flies, dogs, and vultures. The stench was unbearable and there were no sanitation standards of any kind. "Some people just went crazy," Lou says. He reports seeing children even beating up their own parents in hysterical seizures of hunger and fear and hopelessness. There was a significant degree of suicide—this would increase, of course, in the concentration camps that awaited those who survived the ghetto experience.

In desperately small and filthy rooms, eight to ten or more people, from random families, were packed. If a larger room was used, a space that normally would accommodate two or maybe three people, twenty individuals had to endure together. It was standard ghetto practice that from 5:00 p.m. until the following morning, it was *verboten* to venture outside the teeming room.

The tenure in the ghetto did not last long—a few weeks. But to Lou, it felt like an eternity. And it would be the last time and place where he shared space with his parents. As always, he would cope with the unimaginable by regularly turning to God. "It was constantly my oasis," he tells people. "When I would talk with God, especially later in the camps, my heart and my mind would be able to function. Your mind they can't take away from you."

CHAPTER FIVE

The Cookie Factory

All Saints' Episcopal Church, San Diego, California
April 14, 2013

A SOMBER COMMUNITY OF CHRISTIANS AND JEWS GATHERED together at the small but handsome church, its walls filled with stained glass and a number of statue depictions of Jesus on the cross. It was a drizzly Sunday afternoon. Above the rector's lectern, there were still page notations posted for congregants to follow in their prayer books during the recent Easter holiday. Musicians, ministers, a rabbi, and some pulpit guests talked quietly before the 4:00 p.m. commemoration began. Six thick unlit candles, each in a clear vase filled with wax and sorrow, sat upon a simple table in front. They would be lit at the conclusion of the program, each one flickering light for one million of the six million lost Jews.

All Saints' Episcopal Church was hosting a *"Yom Ha-Shoah"* [Holocaust Remembrance Day] gathering in its sanctuary. The featured speaker was Lou Dunst, dressed in a blue suit, with tie and striped shirt, topped with his characteristic yarmulke, there in Christ's house.

The church fell silent as an "organ voluntary" filled the hall with Ernest Bloch's "Four Short Preludes in Memoriam." The cantor from a nearby synagogue sang a piece taken from the Book of Psalms called *"Enosh."* ["Humanity."]

> *Our days are as grass;*
> *We shoot up like flowers that fade*
> *And die as the chill wind passes over them.*
> *Yet your love for those who revere you is everlasting.*
> *Your righteousness extends to all generations.*

Perhaps some of the Jews and Christians wrapped in devotion privately mulled over the scriptural assertion that God's "righteousness extends to all generations." Why would we be here if that were true? How could the divine righteousness not have been extended to the six million Jews slaughtered by the Germans, along with (as Lou Dunst often mentions) an additional six million gypsies, homosexuals, disabled or mentally ill human beings, Jehovah's Witnesses, defiant Catholic priests and clergy of other faiths who spoke out, political opponents, and the innumerable "righteous Gentiles" who fed, protected, or hid Jews?

For those who can see him, Lou Dunst's unimposing and kindly presence, sitting politely and attentively in his pew, offers an alternative layer of healing contemplation. Without saying a word yet, Lou's latent smile, his shining eyes, his slight lean-in of posture, as though he is eager to begin his presentation yet deeply deferential to the setting and protocol—all of these qualities help to soften the general pain, remorse, guilt, and uneasiness of the blended congregation. Lou is survival. Lou is hope. Lou is life.

He never sits down during his more than hour-long soliloquy, not in a high school gym, a federal office, a corporate board room, a community hall, a military installation, or in a church. He will occasionally take a sip of water, treating the little glass or Styrofoam cup like a beatific gift from God that he could never have imagined in four death camps, a ghetto, a running caravan of ghastly, reeking box cars into which he was repeatedly sealed along the rails of hell. He never loses his composure, never weeps, or in any way cloys for special attention or even pity. His story unfailing begins with the declaration, "Holocaust! The murder of six million Jews: the greatest catastrophe to have ever occurred in the history of mankind." He begins with that as a kind of trigger passage for his hawkish memory; yet, he consistently concludes each and every time with his own psalm: "We are all God's children!"

The prayer books in the pews, the hymnals, the blue sheets announcing the program and offering the words of "The Lord is My Shepherd" and "O God Our Help"—even these documents are creased in simultaneous anguish and admiration for the smallish man with the large heart. Lou is survival. Lou is love.

"We were thought by them as being '*Untermentschen*'—sub-human beings," he tells the attentive congregation during the course of his seventy-five minute discourse. In fact, the Germans eventually decided to exterminate not only the "subhuman" Jews, but also the Poles, who were deemed as biologically inferior. This edict would also apply to the vast majority of the Slavic people who, along with the Jews and Gypsies, were defined as *Untermenschen*—hazardous for the Germanic peoples, who represented the Aryan master race. Never before and never since in history has such an application of pure racism been woven into the social science and legislation of any civilized nation.

At the same time, as Lou Dunst testifies, no power group has ever existed like the Nazis—who enjoyed an unparalleled indulgence and extravagance at the physical expense of their victims, who were primarily and overwhelmingly the '*Juden*.'

"They had a situation that was unlike anything ever in history. They used us and abused us. Because they took everything away from us, our belongings, our furniture, our money, our teeth, our shoes, our homes, our paintings, they had whatever they wanted at any time they wanted us. If they needed a goldsmith, they took one of us to be a goldsmith. If they needed a tailor, they made one of us into their tailor. They would scream at us, 'Who is a dentist? Who is a bricklayer? Who is an accountant? Who is a cook?' Whatever they needed, they took one of us for his skills. There was absolutely nothing that they wanted or needed at any time that they did not get immediately and totally. They took it all from us and then they killed us when they were done with what they needed or wanted."

....

After about four weeks in the Mátészalka ghetto, Lou and his family were again thrust into boxcars. "This time it was even worse," he relates. "We were sick and weak and diseased. We had diarrhea and dehydration and the conditions in the rail car—when I talk about it, I can't even believe the things I am actually remembering. Day after day, off we went. We were pressed together like animals. Sometimes the train would stop for hours and hours, and we were gasping for air in the heat, with no light, no water, nothing. They had to stop because the width of the rails did not match the wheels. Or they were hooking up other cars from who knows where? From other cities, even other countries. In the car, some people were dying, some were dead. Some were giving birth but it had to be done in a way that nobody from the Nazis should see; because, like in the ghetto, pregnant woman were shot. If you didn't run fast enough when they wanted you to go from here to there, *boom*! Shot. No questions. No thinking. To them, Jewish life was cheap. Everything they felt like doing, they did it. And always, they were yelling '*Schnell!*' We had to move fast. I saw people, men, women, and children, shot dead in front of me because they didn't move fast enough or they just looked the wrong way. So now, we were again in the box cars. But somehow I believed, that even there, God was in the boxcars."

Then they arrived at a place called Birkenau—though they had no idea where it was or what it was. Birkenau was a small Polish village laid waste by the Nazis in 1939; the name actually derives from the Polish term for a "birch forest." The town was destroyed to make way for the most notorious killing camp in history, Auschwitz. "Auschwitz" is now a historical term synonymous with "extermination."

"There had been no way for us, stuck in the box cars, to even estimate which way we were traveling. We did not know, north, east, south or west, we could not orient ourselves. Few days, few nights, suddenly it stops. Doors are opened and they are shouting: 'Everybody out! Out! *Schnell!*' Everything with them was '*Schnell!*' Fast, fast, fast.

"Some were dying...some were dead...some were giving birth." As always, at this phrasing, Lou's voice softens, almost to a lilt.

"Some were lying in their own excrement.... Some lost their reasoning.... But some of us were able to get out. And we got out and we were met by somber men, wearing those blue, striped, like pajamas—that maybe you've seen in the movies. Maybe ninety-five percent of them, most of them were Jewish people.

"So we talked with them in our language, which was Yiddish. We are trying to find where we are because we have no idea. They say to us, those who would talk, 'Auschwitz!'"

When Lou intones the manner in which the men in striped pajamas, already "residing" in that place declared to them, with grim righteousness, that this was "Auschwitz," he is telling us now that there could not have been any concept in any human mind that such a place could exist. It had to have happened, and people like Lou had to survive it, so that we in its awful legacy can even have a context into which we place it. No wonder he maintains, with absolute faith, "*Ha-Shem* saved me, so that I could tell the story."

As far as Auschwitz meant, remembers Lou, "We had no idea what the word means or where it is, what it is, or what it's supposed to be. They were not allowed to talk to us or tell us what's going on there. One of them got shot right there because they accused them of talking to us. Some of them then told us that we are going to be gassed and cremated. We did not believe them. We thought that these are crazy people. Who would talk like that? What kind of thing was this?"

But the hollow-eyed messengers persisted in their ghastly, matter-of-fact report:

"'You see those chimneys up there? Smoke coming out of there?' We could smell it, yes. Smells like burning flesh or burning hair. But we just knew for sure that nothing like that was going to happen to us because wherever we are coming from, we are decent human beings, taxpayers from wherever we come, we just did not believe that. And we knew that we were not criminals, we didn't do anything, so we just did not believe all of that."

But it was real, and the facts remain the most damning in the history of Europe, if not the entire world. Lou had entered the deepest part of what he often calls "The Black Hole." The purpose, meaning, and definition of Auschwitz are explained succinctly by the encyclopedia of the United States Holocaust Museum:

> The Auschwitz concentration camp complex was the largest of its kind established by the Nazi regime. It included three main camps, all of which deployed incarcerated prisoners at forced labor. One of them also functioned for an extended period as a killing center. The camps were located approximately 37 miles west of Krakow, near the prewar German-Polish border in Upper Silesia, an area that Nazi Germany annexed in 1939 after invading and conquering Poland. The SS authorities established three main camps near the Polish city of Oswiecim: Auschwitz I in May 1940; Auschwitz II (also called Auschwitz-Birkenau) in early 1942; and Auschwitz III (also called Auschwitz-Monowitz) in October 1942.

Nearly one million Jews were murdered at Auschwitz until its liberation by Russian soldiers in January 1945.

The Jews and the gypsies; the homosexuals, disabled, and sundry undesirables; the Russian prisoners of war—they were all collected, crammed into those railroad cattle cars on trains and propelled to Auschwitz. When the trains stopped at Auschwitz II, which was Birkenau, the doors were flung open and the human beings—the mothers, grandmothers, babies, fathers, attorneys, scientists, students, carpenters, rabbis, priests, writers, historians, landscapers, and poets became one massive lump of miserable waste and sub-human litter: they were commanded with venom to release all their meager possessions while still constricted on board. Pulled off, slashed, trampled, slugged, kicked, sometimes shot, those still able were dragged to debark from the train. Lou remembers: unable to stand, dizzy with fear and incomprehension, they assembled, trembling, hysteric, numb, dripping with terror, upon the railway platform, grievously referred to as "the ramp."

And then came perhaps the worst moment. Families, clinging to one another, were abruptly split up—usually forever. Husbands and wives, parents and children, brothers and sisters, without even a millisecond to grieve, reorient, let alone even say good-bye, were torn from another like pieces of paper.

Mechanically, with sinister discipline, an SS officer, typically a Nazi physician, commanded each "unit" into one of two lines. This was a place and a moment barren of any trace of human emotion. Left! Right! This was "the Selection;" a bark from the doctor, sometimes just a directional lift of the thumb, dispatched living persons to their fates. "We had no idea what was happening, why we were there, or what this place was," repeats Lou Dunst over and over again. "People just began to pray. We had no other thing that we could do, even if some of us did not know all the words to the prayer."

There are many accounts that have been written about this horrendous moment of arrival and selection at Auschwitz and many other Nazi extermination camps. One reports it this way:

> Most women, children, older men, and those that looked unfit or unhealthy were sent to the left; while most young men and others that looked strong enough to do hard labor were sent to the right. Unbeknownst to the people in the two lines, the left line meant immediate death at the gas chambers and the right meant that they would become a prisoner of the camp. (Most of the prisoners would later die from starvation, exposure, forced labor, and/or torture.)
>
> Once the selections had been concluded, a select group of Auschwitz prisoners gathered up all the belongings that had been left on the train and sorted them into huge piles, which were then stored in warehouses. These items (including clothing, eye glasses, medicine, shoes, books, pictures, jewelry, and prayer shawls) would periodically be bundled and shipped back to Germany.
>
> The people who were sent to the left, which was the majority of those who arrived at Auschwitz, were never told that they had been chosen for death. The entire mass-murder system depended on keeping this secret from its victims. If the victims had known they were headed to their death, they would most definitely have fought back.

But they didn't know, so the victims latched onto the hope that the Nazis wanted them to believe. Having been told that they were going to be sent to work, the masses of victims believed it when they were told they first needed to be disinfected and have showers.

The victims were ushered into an ante-room, where they were told to remove all their clothing. Completely naked, these men, women, and children were then ushered into a large room that looked like a big shower room (there were even fake shower heads on the walls). When the doors shut, a Nazi would pour Zyklon-B pellets into an opening (in the roof or through a window) which would turn into poison gas once it contacted air.

The gas killed quickly, but it was not instantaneous. Victims, finally realizing that this was not a shower room, clambered over each other, trying to find a pocket of breathable air. Others would claw at the doors until their fingers bled.

Once everyone in the room was dead, special prisoners assigned this horrible task (*Sonderkommandos*) would air out the room and then remove the bodies. The bodies would be searched for gold and then placed into the crematoria.

Those that had been sent to the right during the selection process on the ramp went through a dehumanizing process that turned them into camp prisoners. All of their clothes and any remaining personal belongings were taken from them and their hair was shorn completely off. They were given striped prison outfits and a pair of wooden clogs, all of which were usually the wrong size. They were then registered, had their arms tattooed with a number, and transferred to one of Auschwitz's camps for forced labor.

The new arrivals were then thrown into the cruel, hard, unfair, horrific world of camp life. Within their first week at Auschwitz, most new prisoners had discovered the fate of their loved ones that had been sent to the left. Some of them prisoners never recovered from this news.

Lou Dunst was eighteen years old. He, his brother Irving, and their father Mordecai, were motioned to the right. Priva and their sister Risi were dispatched to the left. "It was the last time I saw my mother," says Lou.

Lou tends to revisit the moments after watching his mother being dragged away, even though he did not realize at that instant that he would never see her again. His refrain is about "the people in the blue, striped pajamas" who whispered to him and the other new arrivals about the smoke emerging from the chimneys "over there," at Birkenau. "Yes, we saw the smoke. They told us, 'You are going to be gassed over there.' We did not believe them. We did not even believe that they believed what they were saying."

The whole report was simply unintelligible to Lou, his brother, and his father.

"We were chased forward. Again, everything was '*Scnhell*!' We never moved fast enough for them. They had their dogs bite us, they hit us over the head. Here we come, in front of Dr. Josef Mengele. He was beautifully dressed, with his big entourage, officers with their beautiful uniforms. Their boots were shined like mirrors. They didn't talk to us. They just shouted, 'You go here, you go there!'"

Lou's mind, blurred with seething mortal fear, looking back in the direction of where his mother and sister had disappeared, somehow remembered a jovial moment back at their home in Jasina. Somebody was having a "*simcha*"—a joyous milestone. Maybe it was a bar mitzvah, maybe a wedding or perhaps a baby naming. He recalled that there was "honey cake and schnapps." Hebrew songs were sung and people were laughing. Then Lou smelled some burning flesh coming through his nostrils, a soldier in his impeccable clothing slammed his rifle butt into Lou's head, and the young man realized that the honey and schnapps were gone forever.

"We were marched on a huge mountain of clothing. We were told to undress completely. We are inquiring, 'Where are all the people from this clothing?' They told us that they went through the chimney. That means that they were cremated. This was the code for gassing and cremation. And the same thing is waiting for us. Of course, we didn't really know right then what was really waiting for us.

"After we got completely undressed, they picked up the strong ones. 'You, you, you, you'—all the strong ones. Stand over there!' They told us that we were going to the cookie factory. All the strong ones. They lied to us. They called it a cookie factory. They lied with a particular brutality. Then they took some of us to work in the *Sonderkommandos*."

Lou was somehow spared this dreadful assignment but he has never forgotten what it was like to even observe the 800 or so unfortunates who got this "privileged duty" all the while knowing that they would categorically be killed—and thus silenced—after a certain interlude at their macabre work.

Sonderkommandos was the title given to death camp inmates whose job was to maintain and service the assembly lines of death. It was a specifically ghoulish circumstance of sadistic treatment: a person got better clothing, more edible food, and even something of a straw mattress in exchange for preparing, coaching, and cataloging thousands upon thousands of other Jews for their deaths in the gas chambers. Some of these individuals, reports Lou, "even had to lie to their own relatives about what was about to happen in the gas chambers and then handle their dead bodies afterwards."

In 2002, the Israeli newspaper, *Ha-Aretz*, ("The Land") published an exposé of the *Sonderkommandos* of Auschwitz-Birkenau.

> [They] arrived in Auschwitz in December 1942. Shortly afterwards, the Germans marched their entire labor team, 200 still relatively healthy and robust men, into a nearby forest. The air was freezing, and snow covered the ground. In the distance they saw and smelt the clouds of smoke emanating from the crematoria, but were still unaware of the terrible truth behind those malodorous clouds. An SS officer, Otto Moll, ordered them to enter a straw-roofed hut in the forest, full of naked bodies. "We saw a mass of naked corpses, men, women and children. We were horror-stricken into an eerie unnatural silence. It took us two days to recover a semblance of normality."
>
> *Sonderkommandos* were divided into several groups, each with a specific specialized function. Some greeted the new arrivals, telling them that they going to be disinfected and showered prior to being sent to labor teams. They were obliged to lie, telling the soon-to-be-murdered prisoners that after the delousing process they would be assigned to labor teams and reunited with their families. These were the only *Sonderkommandos* to have contact with the victims while they were still alive. Other teams processed the corpses after the gas chambers, extracting gold teeth, and removing clothes and valuables before taking them to the crematoria for final disposal.

"We did the dirty work of the Holocaust," said one surviving member of the *Sonderkommandos*. Lou could only agree; his memory works against him when it comes to explaining or describing the chilling predicament of those being among the *Sonderkommandos.*

Sonderkommandos were allocated into several sets. Each team had a unique function. Some were forced to greet the fresh inmates, just thrust off the box-cars. Deceiving them while having their hearts breaking, these Jewish SS slaves conveyed to the new arrivals that they were going to "the shower." Afterwards, they lied, they'd continue on to labor assignments.

Under the pain of their own deaths, these *Sonderkommandos* were compelled to mislead and to subsist without any consciences. Such was the supreme, calculated evil of the Nazis. "They rarely did the deeds themselves," Lou Dunst repeatedly invokes. "They had it done for them."

The *Sonderkommandos*, "95 percent Jewish," says Lou, told the doomed prisoners that after the "delousing" process they would be dispersed to work teams. After that, they'd be reunified with their families. These were the only *Sonderkommandos* to have contact with the victims while they were still alive.

The SS carried out the gassings, and the *Sonderkommandos* would enter the chambers afterward, remove the bodies, manage them and convey them to the crematorium. There were additional, specialized teams that administered the corpses after the group gas chamber murders. Their assignment was to extract gold teeth, confiscate clothing and valuables and then deliver them to the crematoria. This was the "final disposal" of what moments before had been living human beings. The remains were ground to dust and mixed with the ashes. Often enough, an overabundance of ash accumulated; Lou reports that ten to twelve thousand people were gassed and burned daily at Auschwitz-Birkenau. When this happened, the SS would watch over with grim eyes, while the Jewish *Sonderkommandos* would collect the tons of ashes and dump them into the river. It was an industry, a technology, of horror, murder, and waste disposal.[1]

At one session led by Lou Dunst in 2013, a visibly shaken and moved audience member asked Lou Dunst, "What memory sticks out the most for you during your time at Auschwitz?"

"I remember," he answered, "that my mother had rosy cheeks."

---

1   Based upon Sonderkommando, article by Jacqueline Shields, in the Jewish Virtual Library.

CHAPTER SIX

"Like the Stars in the Heaven"

L OU DUNST, THE ULTIMATE SURVIVOR, IS A MAN OF FAITH. BUT that does not mean that he did not fall into deep pits of despair, into his self-described "Black Hole" during his years of internment and dehumanization under the Germans. He is as frank about that as he is direct about his faith, admitting from time to time, "I considered suicide."

It wasn't just a matter of despair. It became a matter of life just being too hard to live, to accept, or to endure. "I want to make it clear about starvation," he often declares. "There is nothing worse, nothing more painful, and nothing that can make people lose their minds. I saw cannibalism in the camps. I saw people eating their dead relatives. There was one section in Mauthausen that was for the Russian soldiers. They were locked in a big box. Just left in there. One day, when the box opened, you could see that they had eaten parts of each other."

The human body is a mechanism that is fueled by an appropriate amount and balance of foods and nutrients. One scientific study maintains the following:

> The body is an effective storage device for fats, nutrients, and other important components. These stores are regulated by nutrition in the form of food, beverages, and vitamin and mineral supplements. When lack of nutrition occurs, the body quite quickly turns to stored reserves, beginning with glycogen, in order to keep vital functions up to par. As the body begins to devour more and more stored components to keep running, the physical effects of starvation become apparent.... By depriving the body of nutrition, starvation slowly allows the body to devour its own reserves, including muscle, fat, and organs, up to the point of complete system shut-down and death.

The Nazis, in Auschwitz, Treblinka, Dachau, Bergen-Belsen, and so many other cities of death and thousands of sub-camps, private murder factories, work-to-death centers, sub-contracted extermination centers, and a variety of slave communities that simply waited for people to succumb to hunger. They then replaced them from the continental-wide boxcar rail system that yielded unimaginable profits to railroad companies such as the Deutsche Reichsbahn (German National Railway of the Third Reich). The process began, continued, and concluded with the death by starvation of a significant number of the six million Jews of the Holocaust. It certainly was the central anguish of those who were alive for any period of time in the death camps over which the smoke and ashes of gassed and then cremated Jews hung, like a smoky layer of hideousness.

"When we were starving," says Lou, "we did things, even to each other, that the mind cannot take into consideration." I remarked to Lou that other survivors have mentioned that the Nazis would enjoy feeding their dogs while forcing the ravenous Jews to watch or even serve them—and their dogs—lavish meals. Lou retorted: "You can train a dog to be a savior or a killer, to be kind or heartless. You can train a man to be either thing, also. But it takes some kind of beast of a human being to not care that another human being is starving to death right in front of you."

Lou has also related a particularly graphic recollection involving starvation. Late one afternoon in the barrack at Auschwitz, he saw a fellow inmate, emaciated and desperate, pick up a handful of vomit from the ground that had been heaved by someone else. The man ingested it.

"I looked at this man, my eyes not taking in what I thought I just saw. I said to him, 'How could you do that? You know, it's maybe dangerous for you. It could kill you.' The man looked at me and asked, 'How long have you been here?' I answered, 'Not so long.' He said, 'When you are here long enough, you won't have to ask why I just did that.'"

Was this the moment when Lou began to contemplate suicide? Or was it sometime before, or was it in the aftermath of that impossibly pitiful incident? Lou doesn't know but he does recall without a doubt that he thought about ending his own life—as so many Jews actually did in the kingdom of death. There were many ways and means, including flinging oneself at the electric fences, hanging, sinking into the sewage, or simply provoking a guard sufficiently to invite an immediate bullet to the head.

In 1986, the US National Institute of Health published a report on this tragic, if fathomable phenomenon: "Suicides in Nazi Concentration Camps." A summation reads:

On the basis of psychiatric interviews with 69 former prisoners of the Auschwitz-Birkenau concentration camp, this paper describes the circumstances, motives, and ways of committing suicide in the camp. The interview made it clear that thousands of prisoners perished by suicide. The number of committed suicides was larger than that of attempted suicides. The most frequent types of suicide victims were prisoners of Jewish descent, foreigners, white-collar workers, and old people. The most common motives of suicides were depressive reactions; anxiety; somatic illnesses; the threat of death; emotional motives; loss of emotional support; beatings and tortures; and patriotic and altruistic motives. The most common methods of committing suicide were flinging oneself onto the electrified wires surrounding the camp, hanging, poisoning, cutting one's veins, and drowning. There were also cases of mass suicides, chiefly in the women's camp. Suicides committed from patriotic or altruistic motives testified to the fact that human beings were able to preserve their dignity even in the face of death.

Lou describes it simply: "Some people lost faith. I thought about suicide, there is no question about it. So like always, I talked to *Ha-Shem*. But first I talked to my parents." His yellow, double-triangular Star of David sewn to his prison shirt like the sorrow woven into his heart, Lou found enough strength and will to look upward and ask the departed Priva and Mordecai, "What shall I do? I cannot live anymore and this is not life. Why, Mother and Father, should I exist just to be tortured, beaten, only to be gassed anyway?"

Lou then shares, with perfect clarity and belief, that "My parents told me that they could not provide me with the answer to such a question. That I should pray to *Ha-Shem* and that he would guide me."

This made sense to Lou as he carried on this heavenly discourse in the midst of hell. So he turned his prayers towards God.

"I prayed to *Ha-Shem* and was told the answer. It would be a sin to commit suicide, He told me clearly, as it would violate The Ten Commandments, 'Thou shalt not murder.' So of course I could not take my own life because that would be murder. I made stronger my commitment to live, no matter what. And I remembered again from *Tehillim* (The Book of Psalms), where it says, 'Let me live, so that I may tell of the deeds of the Lord.' That to me meant, and will always mean, let me live, so that I can tell the story. I am absolutely convinced that *Ha-Shem* saved me and chose to me to survive so that I could tell this story to whoever will be willing to listen. Again, I did nothing heroic in the camps, in the Black Hole. My brother saved my life. If you ask him, he would say to you that I saved his life. But really, I did nothing but try to live. That is why I am here because *Ha-Shem* just happened to pick me to do what I am doing now."

When one listens to Lou, and imagines his death-dance with heaven, a stanza from the Hebrew poet, Avraham Shlonsky, comes to mind:

> *The Sabbath stars have climbed high,*
> *more peaceful than you*
> *who are sad today.*
> *Your sadness is almost blasphemy—*
> *Blowing out the careful candles Mother lit.*

Somehow, starving, despairing, frightened, humiliated, beaten, fighting off lice and typhus and dysentery, seeing things even Satan couldn't imagine, Lou looked up at the stars and he saw and even breathed in his mother's warm challah bread just out of the oven. He smelled the aroma of honey cake and the silky warmth of schnapps slipping down his throat at a *simcha*; he saw his father's work-worn hands delicately folding the mantle over those final three Torah scrolls, his mother's rosy cheeks, and his sister's glowing eyes.

Some of what he literally felt right there in Auschwitz and then later at Mauthausen and Ebensee: his brother Irving unfailingly kept his own hands on Lou's shoulders as they shuffled through the darkness of their journey, as they managed to survive two gas chambers near-misses, and as they were marched and marched through bitter cold nights and days that lacked meaning or direction but during which every minute hurt and scarred and defiled.

"My brother always kept his hands on me from just behind. He never let go of me."

Another parable of the Bible is held in conviction by Lou—the parting of the Red Sea. The Israelites had just fled Egypt in the wake of the Ten Plagues brought down upon the Egyptians. "The Torah is clear about who is doing the freeing," says Lou. "It's not Moses, it's not any person. It was *Ha-Shem*. Moses was just the instrument. The people are told over and over again in the Torah that God will deliver them. This is what I believe. This is what gave me the faith that we would be delivered in the end. In the Torah, God says: 'I will bless you and make your descendants as numerous as the stars in the sky and as the sand on the seashore. Your descendants will take possession of the cities of their enemies.' I always thought about that, too. I asked myself, what God would make such a promise, that we will be like the stars of the sky and then let us disappear now? I remembered that every day and I will remember this to the last day of my life. And I'll remember that my people were up against the waters of the Red Sea and the Egyptians coming in their chariots and *Ha-Shem* said: 'Do not worry. I will deliver you.' And He did!"

And, often enough, with a certain, uncharacteristic militancy, Lou will declare: "None of the nations that ever tried to kill us ever succeeded and none of them are still here. The Nazis, the Romans, the Greeks, the Egyptians, it doesn't matter. We buried them. We are still here and we will always be here. *Am yisrael chai!*" ["The people of Israel live!"]

This is also why a central refrain of this pious, remarkably cheerful, and unalterably kind survivor so loves the modern State of Israel—which he has visited numerous times. "Israel must have secure borders," he thunders. "If we had secure borders back when they were trying to kill every one of us, we wouldn't now be a heap of ashes in Europe."

....

"We were like zombies," says Lou, remembering his experience in Mauthausen. "There really was no such thing as sleep. Going without sleep is worse than going without food. So maybe some of us did sleep but we were told that we were going to the gas chamber. And that's exactly what happened. We were chased into the gas chambers. We were completely naked. When we were in Auschwitz, remember that they were exterminating ten to twelve thousand people every twenty-four hours. Mind-boggling. It was cheap, easy, and fast. They put in something like four thousand people into a warehouse, dropped the Zyklon-B, and within twenty minutes, twenty-five minutes, they were all dead. Now, to take care of so many bodies, the crematoria were running around-the-clock. But they were not sufficient enough. So they had to throw a lot of bodies on a huge mountain of fire. So these people from our group from the—and by the way, not one of them survived from the so-called 'cookie factory'—they took them to drag the extra dead bodies from the gas chambers and to throw them on the mountain of fire."

Ebensee Concentration Camp Ebensee Austria   May 1945

Ebensee Concentration Camp   Ebensee Austria May 1945

Ebensee Concentration Camp Ebensee Austria May 1945

EBENSEE CONCENTRATION CAMP 1945

(PHOTOS TAKEN BY MEMBERS OF ROBERT PERSINGER'S BRIGADE, MAY, 1945)

In preparation for their disposal of the Jews, Lou relates, "our hair was clipped off, everywhere there was hair on our bodies, it was removed. They used our hair, they used whatever they could, they used everything. We were crying for a drop of water, a little food—again and again they told us we don't need any water because we were going to the gas chambers. That's why some people, like me and my brother, were not tattooed. They didn't want to waste any of the materials needed. I was given that number, 68122. Other people were tattooed. It was usually a question of them being useful for the Germans for a while so they were tattooed."

Lou rarely fails to mention the poisonous testimony of the commander of Auschwitz, Rudolf Hoess. "By the way," he mentions, "they were killing us at a rate of ten to twelve thousand a day. But Hoess, when he was in court after the war, he was accused of crimes against humanity, and he was accused of murdering that many people a day, he said, 'Correction! It was not ten to twelve thousand a day. It was sixteen thousand!' He was proud of what he did. It was something very wonderful, very heroic that he felt he accomplished."

When Lou speaks about this, he pauses, and then asks out loud, "Who can describe the feelings of a man like this?"

Rudoph Hoess was not unique among the Nazi leadership: a by-product of the losing end of World War I, frustrated national imperialism and unrequited anger, he emerged from this mélange a ruthless and amoral thug. He was raised in the strict, unforgiving household of a Catholic ex-soldier who instilled in the young Hoess the fanatical belief of duty with an emphasis on sin, guilt and penance. After his experience in the Middle East fighting with the Ottoman Army during WWI, he finished his interrupted secondary education before joining the jingoistic ultra-nationalist paramilitary *Freikorps*, known for terrorizing Jews, Communists, Socialists and other so-called outsiders of the German political and cultural mainstream. It should be no surprise that he would find the Nazi Party attractive; he joined their ranks early, in 1922, after hearing Hitler (another lapsed Catholic) speak in Munich. In this environment he fell in among like-minded angry, disgruntled young men, including Martin Borman, who turned against their religious and moral upbringing to create a frightening system built on hate and violence.

Hoess rose quickly in his new career, joining the SS in 1934 (after being invited by Heinrich Himmler himself, whom he met in 1929 and later, becomes his idol) and working his way through the newly-minted concentration camp system, starting in Dachau. From there, after distinguishing himself as an enthusiastic *Blokfeuhrer*, he served in Sachsenhausen and then on to Auschwitz, where he makes his darkest mark on history. Hoess was instrumental in expanding the Auschwitz camp, originally a transitional facility for prisoners-of-war, into a complex of extermination and forced labor factories for Germany's unwanted *Untermenschen*—namely the Jewish population of all the conquered areas of the mighty Wehrmacht. An apt student, Hoess would discover more and improved methods of eliminating at least 1.1 million people where about 90% of them were Jews. He was famous for destroying his charges with more efficient techniques of mass-murder than ever in history, which included the introduction of gas chambers for speed of execution and crematoria for equally rapid disposal. The outside world, apprised of his depravities upon untold numbers of helpless human beings, turned an unbelieving eye. His braggadocio is not to be ignored; Hoess's claim of killing 16 thousand prisoners per day is a cruel statistic of the magnitude of this state-sponsored horror.

There is no way to properly estimate how many endless thousands of Jews he had exterminated at Auschwitz during his tenure as *kommandant* of the world's most horrific death camp.

However, one life that Hoess did not claim was that of Lou Dunst.

Later on Lou and his brother were hurdled into one of the gas chambers in Mauthausen. "We were pressed together, naked, shrieking with horror, people falling on each other, some trampled, gasping for air, unable to think, function, and even form some kind of final prayer. The noise and the terror was something that the mind cannot even process. We just knew we were about to die by choking to death from poisonous gas. People were pushing, screaming, cutting into each other's skin and faces to the point where the scratches were causing bleeding. Some of us lost our minds right there and then."

But, as Lou will surely reflect and assert, *Ha-Shem* made another miracle. There was a malfunction in the delivery of the Zyklon B tablets (a cyanide-based pesticide) that were to be funneled through the showerheads. Lou and the others miraculously got out from the gas chamber, hysterical, demoralized, relieved, confused, grateful, terrorized, but still not dead.

At one point during his interval at Auschwitz, Lou, a teenager living in hades, approached a fellow inmate that happened to be a Russian officer, not Jewish. The Nazis had a rabid approach to their Soviet prisoners-of-war that rivaled—though never matched—their sadistic conduct against all Jews. It is estimated that during World War II, some 5.7 million Russian soldiers fell into Nazi hands. Their treatment in the camps is generally regarded as being the second most horrifying, only after what the Jews received. The United States Holocaust Museum has published the following summary on this issue:

> Yet for Nazi Germany this attack [the invasion of Russia] was not an "ordinary" military operation. The war against the Soviet Union was a war of annihilation between German fascism and Soviet communism; a racial war between German "Aryans" and sub-human Slavs and Jews. From the very beginning this war of annihilation against the Soviet Union included the killing of prisoners of war (POWs) on a massive scale. German authorities viewed Soviet POWs as a particular threat, regarding them not only as Slavic sub-humans but as part of the "Bolshevik menace" linked in their minds to a Jewish conspiracy.

So there was a kind of grisly affinity between some of the Jewish inmates in places like Auschwitz, Mauthausen, and Ebensee and the many Russian servicemen who also found themselves in these diabolical places. It was not unusual for someone like Lou to interact, if briefly with a Soviet prisoner. Lou Dunst traveled through his "Black Hole," his own purgatory, via the ghetto, in the boxcars time and again, and through these infernal death communities. It was at Ebensee, nineteen years old, with only his brother Irving occasionally able to put his hands on Lou's shoulders that Lou saw a Russian officer seated alone on a stump—in a rare, brief moment of solitude and contemplation. Missing his own father, looking for some kind of insight, some wisp of reason, some paternal comfort, something other than the madness, Lou approached the soldier. "He looked educated, maybe with some wisdom he could give me," remembers Lou.

Lou approached the man, a ranked serviceman but a "sub-human inmate" nonetheless. The tattered coat of his uniform that read the two letters "S. U." that stood for *Sovjetsky Sojuz* assigned to him by the camp authorities barely concealed his withered body and the purplish patchwork of gashes and blows and bruises that discolored his face and hands and that damaged his soul.

Lou asked him: "Tell me, what's going on? What is this? What can it be?"

The Russian looked at him with eyes as empty as death. He said in own language: "My head is not working and my heart is bleeding."

CHAPTER SEVEN

"The Staircase of Death"

Macesz Huszár IS GENERALLY KNOWN AS THE "JEWISH FOOD Bistro" in Budapest, Hungary. It is described in a widely-read travel review as "a new addition to [the city's] District 7's Jewish-style restaurant scene, [which] serves up traditional, home-style Hungarian Jewish dishes in a charming, living room-like milieu." The owner apparently relies upon his Yiddish-speaking grandmother's storied recipes to offer up a variety of delicacies: staples of Jewish cuisine, including matzo-ball soup, *cholent* and traditional Jewish desserts such as *flódni* are on the menu, along with stuffed goose neck and schnitzel. There are goose-skin cracklings and an egg-and-duck liver salad ironically known as "Jewish egg."

There are about 100,000 Jews living in contemporary Budapest—the largest population of Jews in Central Europe. The city is charmingly divided by the luscious banks of the Danube River into "Buda" and "Pest." Seventy years after the Holocaust, there is no shortage of synagogues, Hebrew academies, Jewish wine bars, art galleries, and community centers. The city is home to one of the most striking and regal synagogues in the world—*Dohány Utcai Zsinagóga*, The Dohány Street Synagogue, with its unforgettable arches, Moorish façade, twin towers, gilded, onion-shaped domes, small-rose windows, and ubiquitous eight-pointed stars. This is the synagogue that, as mentioned earlier, the Nazis converted into a stable during their occupation of Hungary.

But listen to the conversations taking place among the soup-eating, smartphone-bearing Jews in the *Macesz Huszár* delicatessen and the others gazing at artifacts in the Dohány Street Synagogue and its attached Jewish Museum. A seven-year restoration of the historic temple culminated in 1998 and people do remark about and praise this end-of-century milestone. But they also worry and talk frankly among themselves about another, unwelcome restoration: open, even violent anti-Semitism in Hungary that has also triggered several vicious incidents in and around the synagogue. Even while relaxing at the delicatessen and taking in beer and pastrami, Jews ruminate about the fact that Dohány Street was the border line of the Jewish Ghetto imposed by the Germans and earnestly maintained by the Hungarians.

"The Hungarians were the worst," declares Lou Dunst repeatedly, when it came to brutality, sadism, and mass murder. "Even worse than the Ukrainians, which is hard to accomplish." His assessment is underscored in that today's Hungary; more Jews are contemplating or undertaking emigration than at any time since the end of World War II. The MIÉP–*Jobbik* Third Way Alliance of Parties, a neo-Nazi coalition, has gained a notable presence in the national political discussion and its members receive startlingly high votes in local and parliamentary elections, winning 17% in 2010. *The Jewish Forward* put it simply: "*Jobbik* ran on a populist platform that attacked incompetent Hungarian officials, Roma [gypsy] 'criminals' and nefarious Israeli businessmen who were accused of buying up Hungary." [2]

Ominously, "*Jobbik*" means "The Movement for a Better Hungary," meaning better without Jews. A prominent Chabad rabbi named Shlomo Koves moved from Paris to Budapest in the 1990s. One of the reasons for his move is that he had grown tired of the frequent physical assaults he endured in the French capital. But now in Budapest, he girds himself when walking to his *shul* on Saturday morning for the constant flow of verbal attacks, including cries of "Dirty Jew!" and "Hungary belongs to Hungarians!"

A leading American newsmagazine described the old/new anti-Semitic narrative of Hungary that corroborates Lou Dunst's understandably cheerless assessment of that nation:

> In June [2012], Budapest's retired chief rabbi, Jozsef Schweitzer, was accosted by a man who said he "hates all Jews." In October, two men attacked Jewish leader Andras Kerenyi, kicking him in the stomach and shouting obscenities at him. When Kerenyi's assailants were arrested, an online radio station praised the attack, calling it "a response to general Jewish terrorism." In December, Balazs Lenhardt, an independent Member of Parliament, burned an Israeli flag in front of the Hungarian Foreign Ministry during an anti-Zionist protest — one in which participants shouted, "To Auschwitz with you all." In the past several months, Jewish cemeteries have been vandalized, Holocaust monuments have been damaged, and swastikas have been painted on synagogue walls.

---

2   *The Forward*, May 3, 2013.

> On March 14, professors at Eotvos Lorand University in Budapest found stickers affixed to their office door that read, "Jews! The university belongs to us, not you! Regards, the Hungarian students."

Isolated anti-Jewish events occur occasionally throughout Europe, but the frequency of these incidents in Hungary has accompanied a measurable darkening of public opinion. Andras Kovacs, a sociologist at Budapest's Central European University, found that from 1992 to 2006, levels of anti-Semitism in Hungary remained relatively stable. About 10% of adults qualified as fervent anti-Semites, another 15% had some anti-Semitic feelings, and 60% of the population was not anti-Semitic at all. But beginning in 2006, when Hungary's economy began to deteriorate and far-right parties began to rise, the intolerance started to intensify. By 2010 the percentage of those who qualified as fervent anti-Semites had risen to as high as 20%, and the percentage who said they held no anti-Jewish feelings had dropped to 50%.[3]

"They had a riot just a few years ago," says Lou, "right at the Great Synagogue in Budapest. They were throwing stones at it and yelling "Jews get out!' In the war, again I tell you, they [the Hungarians] were the worst evil people. More than anybody else. More than the Ukrainians…. Remember, [Adolf] Eichmann's[4] headquarters were there, right there in Budapest. They hung Hannah Senesh there, that wonderful Jewish girl who parachuted from Israel where she was free and joined the freedom partisans. It wasn't the Germans who tortured and hung her. It was the Hungarians themselves. I don't know why they were like that but it's just true. So of course it's happening again now in Hungary."

The *TIME* article also states, in concert with Lou's statements and feelings:

> Hungary's history of anti-Semitism is long and sadly not that unusual — especially among other Central and East European countries. Even before it joined with Nazi Germany in World War II, Hungary established a quota limiting the number of Jews in

---

3   From *TIME* Magazine, April 1, 2013

4   The Nazi SS-*Obersturmbannführer* (Lieutenant Colonel) considered the principal manager of the Holocaust. Because of his organizational talents and ideological reliability, Eichmann was assigned the task of facilitating and managing the logistics of mass deportation of Jews to ghettos and extermination camps in German-occupied Eastern Europe. He was the singular Nazi caught by Israeli agents (in Argentina), brought to trial in Israel, and executed there in 1962. Israel has no capital punishment; this remains its only exception throughout its entire existence.

certain professions. An estimated 560,000 of the country's 800,000 Jews perished in the Holocaust and another 20,000 left during the 1956 revolution. Under communism, public religious expression was banned and anti-Semitic sentiment dropped off, but it began rising again in 1990 after the [Soviet-backed] regime fell.

With reference to the experience of his lifetime in Europe, Lou Dunst may single out the Hungarians for their German-fed barbarism, but he is consistent on the overall theme: "The Nazis themselves rarely did the dirty work. They had the Europeans, our neighbors in Czechoslovakia in the beginning, do it for them. And they were always very willing and excited to do it. Even in the camps, we did not see so many Germans in uniforms. They had Slavs, Czechs, Hungarians of course, and always the Ukrainians do the most brutal and sadistic things to us. These people were also under the Nazis, of course. But they didn't mind keeping themselves alive, maybe even earning a little money or some special privileges for taking out their hatred for us, which they also had, directly on us. We were really alone, without any sympathy from anybody, and the Nazis just ran the show. I am saying things to you about what these people did to us, the beatings, the mass killings, the burning of our synagogues while we were still locked up in them, the raping of our mothers and sisters and daughters, and even though I was there and saw it, I cannot believe what I am actually remembering."

Lou reflects heavily on the particularly agonizing question of the "kapos." A *kapo*, meaning "prisoner functionary," was an inmate in the camps with the most despicable job assignment that brutally revealed that darkest and most cynical mindset of the SS murder organization. Some of these *kapos* were Jews and they inflicted direct, even animalistic treatment upon other Jews just to retain their special, even privileged status. The SS/*kapo* hierarchal arrangement was a particularly clear manifestation of Lou Dunst's insistence that history understand a central fact of the Holocaust culture: the Germans, in their glistening boots and plush quarters, did not usually do the filthy, hands-on work of their genocidal industry. It was, day-to-day, night-to-night, handled by others, including Jews who were caught between obeying the most gruesome of orders or delivery to their own immediate deaths.

The *kapos*, viscerally despised and feared by regular Jewish prisoners, were consigned by the SS guards to supervise forced labor or carry out administrative tasks in the camp. They beat, kicked, whipped, sodomized, and basically extended the macabre concepts of the Nazis into the barracks, gas chambers, and crematoria of Jewish reality. They did it in exchange for amnesty from hard labor, for non-convict clothing, and for the "luxury" of a private room. At best, they did it in order to survive. At worst, they did it because they themselves were beasts. In theory, the Nazi design here was to create another ghastly dimension to their Final Solution of the Jewish Question: the enforced pitting of Jew against Jew within the lethal box of the concentration camp culture.

ARMBAND OF A JEWISH KAPO

Many of the *kapos*, both Jews and non-Jews, were actual criminals who had been busted out of the jails of their respective nations when the organized chaos of the Nazis swept into Poland, Czechoslovakia, Hungary, Rumania, France, Denmark, Finland, and elsewhere. Some of them (usually not the Jewish *kapos*) were granted paroles in exchange for performance that especially pleased their SS lords.

The Jewish Virtual Library succinctly summarizes the emotional and physical oppression and entrapment of the Nazi *kapo* system:

> Certain camps even had a hierarchy: *Oberkapo, Kapo, Unterkapo.* Initially, *Kapos* were appointed from the ranks of ethnic German prisoners convicted on criminal charges. These criminals enjoyed extra privileges of great importance under camp conditions: better food, clothing, and housing. In return, many of them tyrannized the prisoners with a cruelty equal to that of the SS, motivated both by the desire to curry favor among the SS as well as by sadistic inclinations. In the course of time, the political prisoners in many camps succeeded in ousting some of the criminals and having them replaced by *Kapos* from their own ranks. Jews were appointed *Kapos* only in those camps which were all Jewish. Some *Kapos* exercised their power humanely and sensitively and worked

to assist their fellow prisoners.[5] Others mimicked the oppressive behavior of the SS and may have indeed internalized their values. Thus, the term *Kapo* became synonymous with a cruel and egocentric person who oppresses, tortures, and exploits others.

"My *kapo* was a criminal," says Lou, recalling his tenure in Ebensee. "He was not normal. He killed his own family. Remember, the Nazis were not in the camps"—Lou emphasizes this fact repeatedly and passionately. "All the bad things that were done in the camps were done by inmates. There were the *kapos*, for example. Some of the torture was done by them. Of course, they were told to do it, they didn't all love doing it. Some of them were real criminals; some of them were just sadistic. My *kapo* was a criminal. Not Jewish. He was taken out of a jail where he was sentenced to life and he became a *kapo*. That was the arrangement. In other words, these *kapos*, they were our foremen, they were our teachers, they were 'the top.' They were our commanders, our leaders. That's how it worked. It was a civilization of criminals. The Germans just watched over it. Those of them that maybe were not criminals became criminals. Even Jewish *kapos*, they became criminals. It was a very bitter issue. Very hard. They did things to us that were unbelievable. We didn't see the Nazis much at all. These *kapos* we saw and suffered from day in and day out. That's how the Nazis arranged it."

Lou also allowed that, upon liberation in the various camps, revenge was taken against many of the *kapos*. They were murdered, strangled, cut apart or even poisoned by some of the frenzied inmates who could no longer contain their cosmic rage and feelings of betrayal—particularly against the *kapos* who were Jews. As mentioned in the opening chapter of this book, Sgt. Robert Persinger recalled seeing the slaughtered bodies of *kapos* strewn about the Ebensee extermination camp in the aftermath of the American liberation on May 6, 1945.

Lou reflects, somberly: "Some of us couldn't contain ourselves...the blood was boiling, the hatred: why did this happen to us? And how could these *kapos* be so sadistic and cruel to us and they weren't even Germans?"

The Nazis didn't only kill humans; they killed human spirits.

Not long after the Germans seized Austria in 1938, a group of top-ranking SS and Gestapo officers took a ride to a site near the villages of Mauthausen

---

5   This fact, that some of the kapos, if only a minority, risked their well-being on behalf of their detainees, must not be overlooked by history.

and Gusen in the upper section of the country. It was about twelve miles east of the city Linz. Within weeks, a series of ruthlessly brutal labor-death camps and sub-camps were created, collectively known as Mauthausen and literally built for and upon the massive granite quarries in the area. The Nazis referred to this camp cluster as *Knochenmühle*—"the bone-grinder."

On August 8, 1938, prisoners from the Dachau concentration camp (one of the very first; located within Germany) were transferred to the Wienergraben quarry. The construction of Mauthausen was inaugurated. Besides being the site of the most merciless work/murder centers in history, the camp and its 49 sub-camps were managed by a lethal amalgamation of SS officers and industrial businessmen who understood the profit-value of slave labor. The general site was leased, during the course of crisp commercial discussions, from the city of Vienna. A number of well-known German banks underwrote the project with loans and grants and contracts for shared revenues: the sub-humans working the quarries would produce and provide the materials needed for major architectural plans—the repaving and rebuilding of major cities throughout the new German continent.

Lou Dunst and his brother Irving, having survived the Auschwitz gas chambers, became two meaningless human dots in the grand collage of the Aryan empire rising speedily in Europe.

The eminent British-Jewish historian Martin Gilbert has written about a fateful conference that took place at Mauthausen in March of 1944. Adolf Eichmann called together his immediate subordinates for a conference on the grounds of the quarried annihilation camp. The agenda: the deportation of Hungary's 750,000 Jews—many of whom (notably from the professional circles) would be removed to Mauthausen.

How to effectively arrange for this mass action? Rely upon the Hungarians themselves, of course. As he had in the past, Hitler himself called upon the very cooperative Regent of Hungary, Admiral Miklós Horthy, to the plush Klessheim Castle outside Salzburg, Austria. The Admiral, whose nation was formally a part of the Axis, complied with the directive. He specifically agreed to promptly deliver 100,000 Jewish slave laborers for the war effort.

The very next day, the Germans initiated action against Hungary's Jewish communities, "arresting two hundred Jewish doctors and lawyers, their names chosen at random from the Budapest telephone book. All were deported to Mauthausen."[6]

---

6   From Martin Gilbert's *The Holocaust: A History of the Jews of Europe During the Second World War*. New York: Holt, 1985

Lou Dunst is never reticent about the fact, in his words, that "I am uneducated. I was kicked out of school as a youngster, not because I was a bad boy. I was Jewish. I never went to college." Although he tells his Holocaust story while making references in several languages, including Yiddish, Russian, German, and Czech, he claims that he has mastered no single language (he is modest and self-deprecating about his fluent English). Indeed, Lou is no physician, attorney, or scientist. He is a survivor. The fact that, for whatever reason, the Nazi syndicate sought to imprison and kill off Jewish "professionals" is as much an irony for Lou as it is mysterious for all sane people. Yet the introduction of sanity into any discussion of the Holocaust is itself insane.

It was in the aftermath of Eichmann's staff meeting at Mauthausen and Hitler's coffee and cake with the Hungarian Regent Horthy that Lou and Irving arrived at Mauthausen and endured its infamous steps. A paradigm of the kind of ruthlessness that Lou and Irving survived at Mauthausen is also described by Martin Gilbert in his massive scholarship on the Holocaust: Deportees from other camps, such as Buchenwald and Auschwitz who arrived at Mauthausen were immediately enslaved "in the punitive stone quarries, hauling massive blocks of stone up a steep incline. As they climbed the 148 steps, they were whipped and beaten." (Other accounts placed the number of steps of "the staircase of death" at 186.)

Lou also reports seeing guards summarily machine-gunning down the terrified climbers—with random and rabid hilarity. He not only saw it; he feared it, even as he struggled to lug the stones and blocks and iron pieces that were thrust upon him in the glaring open exposure of these dreaded steps. The Jews were forced to push unbearably heavy carts, most of them weighing over 100 pounds. Many lost their footing and just fell to their deaths under these loads.

From time to time, some of the climbers, referred to by the Germans as "parachutists," would simply join hands and leap to their deaths in collective suicide. When this began to happen too often, the inmates were placed under an even heavier reign of sadism. In his 1945 book called Mauthausen, published in Paris, Paul Tillard reports about two particularly abominable guards who enforced the merciless surveillance. There was a woman known as "the blonde fraulein" and a man called "Hans the Killer." The longtime commander of Mauthausen was a bestial officer, SS *Sturmbannführer* Franz Ziereis, who was nicknamed "Babyface" by the prisoners. Ziereis attempted to flee the death camp in 1945 but was tracked and shot dead by American soldiers. The

GIs then allowed vengeful Jewish inmates to hang the corpse in the middle of his former domain.

When one takes in Lou's heartrending accounts of his journey through hell, whose coordinates range from the Mátészalka ghetto through the boxcars ("I was an experienced traveler") to Auschwitz-Birkenau to Mauthausen to Ebensee, one is thoroughly convinced that this kindly, loving man is both telling the truth and hoping to clean the hearts of his listeners. He simply wants people to stop judging, defaming, and disliking one another, saying, with an almost unbearably poignant tone, "We don't need any more war. We don't need any hatred. God has given us a beautiful earth with enough food for all of us to share and to love one another. Why fight with each other?"

In fact, the narrative that Lou shares, though beyond reproach, almost requires corroboration—if just for the reason that, as Lou himself confesses, "I am telling you things that I remember seeing but my mind is not believing these things that I am actually remembering."

In a parallel accounting of the indescribable goings-on at Mauthausen, a historian reports about the plight of a group of Dutch Jews:

> They arrived in Mauthausen on June 17, 1941. A batch of fifty was immediately killed: "They were chased naked from the bathhouse to the electrified fence." The others were murdered in the main quarry of the camp, the "Vienna Ditch." According to [a] witness, these Jews were not allowed to use the steps leading to the bottom quarry. "They had to slide down the loose stones at the side, and even here many died or were severely injured. The survivors then had to shoulder hods [troughs carried over the shoulder for transporting loads, as of bricks or mortar], and two prisoners were compelled to load each Jew with an excessively heavy rock. The Jews had to then run up the 186 steps. In some instances the rocks immediately rolled downhill, crushing the feet of those that came behind. Every Jew who lost his rock in that fashion was brutally beaten, and the rock was hoisted onto his shoulders again. Many of the Jews were driven to despair the very first day and committed suicide by jumping into the pit. On the third day the SS opened the so-called 'death gate,' and with a fearful barrage of blows drove the Jews across the guard line,

the guards on the watchtowers shooting them down in heaps with their machine guns.... The barracks were 'cleared' of Jews... in barely three weeks. Every one of the 348 prisoners perished by suicide, or by shooting, beating, and other forms of torture. When asked how the Dutch Jews had adapted to the hard work, Commandant Ziereis answered: "Ah, hardly a one is still alive."[7]

Lou Dunst regularly highlights the complete isolation of the Jews of Europe, the lack of compassion (to say the least) or the dark disinterest of the countless people who knew or even saw what was going on and did nothing. (In fairness, and true to his good heart, he does pay tribute to the "righteous gentiles" who fed, hid, or secretly transferred Jews to safety—always at their own mortal risk). But even Lou cannot excuse the duplicity, the willing and fervent cooperation, of the overwhelming majority of Europeans who found exhilarating release for their own virulent anti-Semitism via the Nazi war against the Jews.

The same historian who documented the Dutch story above also uncovered a shameless example of eyewitness dispassion adjacent to Mauthausen:

> German populations were also quite well informed about the goings-on in the concentration camps, even the most deadly ones. Thus, people living in the vicinity of Mauthausen, for example, could watch what was happening in the camp. [One witness] sent a letter of complaint to the Mauthausen police station: "In the concentration camp Mauthausen at the work site in Vienna Ditch inmates are being shot repeatedly; those badly struck live for yet some time, and so remain lying next to the dead for hours or even half a day long. My property lies upon an elevation next to the Vienna Ditch, and one is often an unwilling witness to such outrages. I am anyway sickly and such a sight makes a demand on my nerves that in the long run I cannot bear. I request that it be arranged that such inhuman deeds be discontinued, or else done where one does not see it."[8]

---

7   From *Saul Friedlander's The Years of Extermination: Nazi Germany and the Jews, 1939–1945.* New York: Harper, 2007.

8   Friedlander quoting from Gordon J. Horwitz' *In the Shadow of Death: Living Outside the Gates of Mauthausen* (New York, 1990).

When I asked Lou about this report, he lifted his shoulders in submission to what he knows is the glaring truth of history, smiled ruefully, and simply said: "Well of course people knew, they saw, they heard. Many of them were very happy about it and the Nazis had no problem recruiting them to help kill us. We ourselves didn't know who could see, who could not see. All we saw was people from every country where the Nazis came jumping in and helping and telling them 'Good job!'"

Lou narrates his own passage into the horrifying world of Mauthausen. But first he invokes the messianic hope that is part of his heart-essence: "Sometimes, people would resist what the Germans would tell them to do. Normally, if we said no, or if we tried to resist in any way: *GGGRRRRRRR!*"—Lou points his right index finger and waves it back and forth to recall the grind of a machine gun.

"But others would try to gain an extra moment, an extra second. They kept thinking and praying: what if THIS is the moment that the *meshiach* will come? Why not? We've been waiting for the *meshiach* for as long as we've been around. Why not that it should happen right then, at the worst possible moment? Because we are still waiting for the *meshiach*, the messiah. Including myself.... I was looking up all the time, asking, is the messiah coming?" Lou pauses and wets his lips, his eyes moistening just a little. In the hall where he is speaking, there is a profound silence. Not one soul in the room, Jew, Christian, is unaware of the sense that the messiah is at least...listening.

"Some miracle happened," Lou repeats, "and we were not gassed at Auschwitz. Next thing we know, we are at the railroad again. Back into the boxcars. This time, it was different. Because there were no women, no children, no sick people. Just young men, from 15, 16, on up to maybe 40–42. Off we go: *chook-chook*. Before we know anything, we are in MAUTHAUSEN." Lou always pauses and clearly enunciates the names of Nazi places and identities of Nazi officers he encountered. "Yes, it's MAUTHAUSEN."

He reminds his listeners that "Mauthausen was famous already—or infamous, whichever way you like to view it. It was famous for the bad things that they were doing there. Torture, beatings, sexual tortures, things that may not even be in the dictionary. Just to give you a little for-instancehow they interrogated there. A Russian general was interrogated there by the name of Gorbachev.[9] They tortured him to death. After the war was over, the Soviet government came in and they put up a monument explaining what was happening there. There are other monuments there, too."

---

9   No relation to the future Soviet Premier Mikhail Sergeyevich Gorbachev.

Lou exhorts his audiences to go to Mauthausen in Austria today and comprehend it personally. It's as if he wants or requires them to grasp that these events are not ancient history—it just happened and the evidence is still there. "If you are ever close to Budapest, close to Vienna, close to Prague, go over there and see it. The wooden barracks are not there anymore, but most of it—we built it—was built with stone. So it will be there for a long time."

Lou's testimonies about "the bone-grinder" of Mauthausen and the diabolical satellite camp Ebensee that followed for him—all the bitter harvest of his memories—will also be there for a long time.

CHAPTER EIGHT

"We Have to Stay Away from the Cruelty"

I F GOD EVER NEEDED VERIFICATION FROM A HUMAN BEING, GOD need only check in with the soul of Lou Dunst. Here follows just a partial inventory of Lou's living values—a kind of "little Talmud" that lines the heart of a man who saw the worst and believes in the best; who survived the ashes and turned them into a fire of love.

There have been a number of instances in Lou's life, particularly after the war (as we shall see), when Lou had to be a recipient of a modest credit from a prospective employer or business partner—or simply call upon their trust. "I would have nothing, no money, nothing at all to offer. But I promised the person that, even if I have to come back and scrub the floors and clean out the toilets, I would absolutely make good and pay everything back."

The record shows that, without exception, Lou kept his promises and often returned more than was given to him. "I learned it as a boy, growing up, from my mother and father. The love of the family has always given me the values that I will live by till the day I die." Lou recalls the "little extra" his father allowed on the store scale when a customer needed a bit more cornmeal, some additional bread, or just some credit. He certainly remembers the over-sized lunches his mother would pack for him just so he could share something with a hungry classmate—and not make a fuss about it.

He thought about these quiet matters of justice, even agonized over them, in the midst of the death camp culture.

"I would see my brother from time to time. Maybe once in a week or two weeks. I was number 68122 and he was 68123. If he was able to get next to me in a line, or when they had us just walk for miles and miles for no particular reason, or during the morning roll call (the prisoners would be forced to stand still in the cold, heat, rain, or snow for hours while the guards methodically called out each and every one of their names), he would put his hands on me whenever he could. The family unity kept us alive. I say that he saved my life and if he were still here, he'd be telling you that I saved his life." (Irving Dunst died in 2012).

But then there was the time when Lou encountered Irving between a rusted barbed wire railing and Irving carefully, hurriedly, at risk to both of them, passed a piece of bread to his younger brother. It was, at best, a moldy piece, certainly not clean or fresh—a far cry from the rich, warm challah bread that emerged from the sweet oven of their dear mother back in Jasina. But it was some scant meager sustenance nonetheless, a darkened, desperate bit of "nourishment" that had spent time in dirty pockets and had been likely bartered for something else. The only ovens that applied to this location were the ones cremating Jews, Slavs, and Russians nearby. The crumbled excuse for a slice of bread nonetheless represented a momentary, fleeting bit of relief from the prevailing, unyielding, mind-bending starvation that was as much a part of the two boys' screamingly harsh existence as the smell of burnt flesh in the air. And the exchange of it between the two boys could verily cost them their lives if the wrong person saw or reported it.

And still Lou struggled with it, philosophically and from the point of ethics. He said: "I kept thinking later, how could I take that piece of bread from my brother? So maybe I got a little something for my hunger but where does that leave him? I should have refused it and let him take it."

It is a tribute to Lou's value system and teaching principles, derived from his Jewish family upbringing that such a dissertation would even play out in the mind of a teenager living in the netherworld. It recalls the eminent Talmudic declaration, found in The Ethics of the Fathers: "In a place where there are no human beings, you be a human being!"

Did Lou develop these precepts because of a seminar or a group dialogue among detainees in the ghetto or a discussion between inmates at Auschwitz, Mauthausen, or Ebensee death camps? No, not at all. In fact, he tells people when they inquire, that there was rarely much discourse among the prisoners in these places. They were all from different locations and now thrown together into an environment that was cruel and terrifying beyond imagination. Each person, child, woman, man, coped privately and many did not cope at all. They lost any semblance of reasoning or logic or comprehension. "What was I going to say to the next man?" repeats Lou. "He was cold, I was cold. He was hungry, I was hungry."

In fact, Lou will occasionally, painfully share his recollections of the indescribable things the wretched inmates did to each other—for food or for warmth. Some of the *kapos* or Scribers abused the very young children for sexual gratification. "They [the Nazis] dehumanized us so that we even treated each other sometimes like animals."

No, Lou Dunst—who ascribes his survival and sanity to the serendipitous presence of his brother Irving in the camps with him—did not garner his life's teaching principles, his moral equation, his "little Talmud" from other people. They were all trapped in a private abyss and they actually had little to say to one another.

Lou Dunst developed his spiritual curriculum because of his private relationship with God and from the belief that he, Lou, was chosen specifically to live. "God was in the boxcars" was not the majority opinion of the doomed Jews of the Holocaust. It remains the decidedly special doctrine of Lou Dunst.

There was an occasion when Lou spoke to a community middle school of truant youngsters; he described it, with a twinkle in his eye as "I am going to speak with the bad boys." Even with this affectionate depiction, Lou reveals his intrinsic forgiving nature and his inability to categorize or lump people together because of their ethnic, racial, or demographic backgrounds. Besides, after what Lou experienced in Europe, he knows all too well who "the bad boys" really are.

The young men—and several women—were transfixed. About forty of them, many of them Hispanic, truly lacking normal home lives and the material things that American teens take for granted, were engrossed by this unimposing man with a yarmulke, an accent, a smile, and an unbelievable story. Not a single one of the students was Jewish. There was no cultural bridge between Lou and them but Lou built one upon the beams of humanity.

In a different setting, this group of societal castaways, with their brash dark clothing, their assortment of bling, their earrings (males and females), wide belts, and punk hairstyles, might have been perceived as dangerous by a visiting lecturer. Lou does not fear anyone—these were just a bunch of kids who, like him, were outcast from the greater civilization (though hardly to the genocidal point that Lou suffered through in Europe). Lou looks at people and all he sees are souls. People look at him and they are disarmed by his candor, sweetness, vulnerability, and capacity to punch through to their consciences without any video or cellular devices and with only words and the enduring power of a story.

After his discourse, Lou invited questions, as he typically does. "You can ask me anything about any subject. Nothing is inappropriate! If nobody has anything to ask, I'll fall asleep!"

One young man wanted to know, "All together, how many days did you travel in those boxcars?"

Lou answered: "I have no way of knowing how many days it was lasting in there. I just don't know. I traveled four times in boxcars, you get in those boxcars, no food, no water, no toilets. It was frightening. We could not even concentrate on what was happening to us…One time they told us that they are going to 're-settle' us. We just didn't know. ..Each and every trip, I guess, was approximately three, four days and three, four nights. It took longer than it should have because of their stop-and-go, stop-and-go to hook up other boxcars."

The feeling of disbelief rose in the room. Not one of the students had even given a passing thought to their cellular phones for well over an hour.

Another pupil asked: "How many days did you go without food or water?"

"Different times it was changed; it was not always the same. But you'd be surprised how a human being can go for a long time without, but the thirst was more difficult than the hunger. It was burning. The mouth was so dry that the tongue didn't move. I couldn't swallow because it was all dry. I need to tell you that sometimes things happened in the transports that no sane human being can believe. They would come to a stop and out came the people from the villages nearby, the civilians. And the Jewish people in the boxcars were crying out for water, just some water. This was in Poland. So the Jewish people said, we will give you money just to have some water. The Polish villagers said, we don't want money for the water, we want gold, we want your jewelry. So the Jewish people gave them their gold and their jewelry and the villagers ran off with all of it but still didn't give them any water."

The school room fell into the numbness of a morgue. Lou continued: "This is how cruel they were. And this why we now have to stay away from the cruelty. Stay away from the hatred. Love! We should love each other and help each other."

Now a student asked: "How did you survive what you went through?"

"Very good question. The most important answer would be God. I was in Auschwitz and we were being killed. There was nothing much to say to any other prisoner. What was there to talk about? Also, our minds were not functioning. So I said to myself, I'm going to talk to God. He will listen to me, He is always available, the line is never too busy. So what am I going to say? Here I'm going to talk to the King of all kings, the Judge of all judges, I better be careful what I'm saying. So I said, 'Dear God, let me live so that I can tell the story….' So here I am now obligated to tell you the story, as long as I can. That is what I learned from talking with God."

A teacher asked, are there similarities between Germany then and the United States now? Lou responded by declaring, "Well, it's happening in certain parts of the world. I've been to Africa several times. I went with my wife. And we see that people are today killing people there without even knowing why they are killing. For no reason. And actually (Lou's voice now in crescendo) there is no reason why a man should kill another man! God is giving us this beautiful world, there is plenty of food for all of us, and we don't need to kill each other. We need to love each other! We each have to start with our own hearts (he points to this chest), here in our own hearts. We have to clean our hearts. And we have to look around us and have peace at home, peace in the city, in the school. We have to learn how to live like brothers and sisters BECAUSE WE ARE BROTHERS AND SISTERS, no matter where we came from and where we are going. We are God's children."

"Go and see Mauthausen," Lou again exhorts yet another audience. "We built it from stone and it is a gold mine for Austria because people are coming there to visit, night and day." He describes the 186 steps: "You can see it; there are pictures available of that." He wants to be sure that if the listener was not going to personally travel to the site, then he or she should "look it up."

As a living voice much more haunting than the written record, Lou relates: "We had to run up those steps. We didn't have the strength to walk. Those that couldn't keep up with the tempo, they tripped and fell down and were trampled to death. So some of us made it into the camp and some did not."

Lou and Irving made it—not without witnessing and trying to blink through the torrent of falling Jews, shot Jews, and already some Jews just leaping into the rocks below to end their misery.

"Here comes nighttime," he continues. "The chief of the barracks says, 'Everybody is going to sleep.' We look at each other. We look around. Nothing looks like sleeping. No beds, no bunks, no mattresses, no blankets, nothing that relates to sleeping! And he continues, 'Every one of you will take up this much room. (Lou demonstrates with his hands: an absurdly tiny amount of space for a human being to consider sleeping in.) We had no idea what he's talking about. But he knew. He says, 'Like this and like this and like this.' (Lou animatedly demonstrates now with his hands what appear to be impossibly small, packed rectangles of space. The listener begins to understand that the guard was directing the Jews to sleep essentially folded sideways into each other.) "And the guard says, 'Yes, like Portuguese sardines.' I don't know why he used the example of Portuguese sardines but that's what he said. We still did not know what exactly he wants us to do. He demonstrated, he stretched himself out. 'Take up this room, on one side straight.' And his feet were in somebody else's face and somebody else's feet were in his face. It was ridiculous. You couldn't turn, you couldn't breathe. Maybe some of us did sleep because we had gone for quite some time without sleep. We had gone without food, without water, without anything. But the worst was without sleep. Without sleep, we were like zombies.

"So maybe some of us did sleep. But we were crying for some food, for some water. And we were told there's nothing to worry about because we are going to the gas chamber."

....

Back at the middle school where Lou addressed "the bad boys" in 2013:

A youngster, of particular intelligence and sensitivity, suggested to Lou that, while nothing in the world has ever happened at the level of what the Nazis did to the Jews and the various other categories of sub-humans, "this kind of stuff is still happening all around the world." The student mentioned the proliferation of gun violence, even wholesale massacres, taking place regularly in American schools, malls, and cinemas. Another one jumped in and referred to the genocide of Rwanda in the 1990s. "People don't seem to have learned the lesson." What did Lou think?

"Yes, we are still in a black hole," said the survivor of death camps and boxcars. "I know that little children are coming into the schools right now and they are killing each other. It's for what? Nothing! I was in a black hole and I crawled out. But we have to crawl out now together—we don't have to just lie down on the couch and remain in the black hole for the rest of our lives. We have to reform ourselves. We have to get education. We have to become clean and decent human beings. There's no limit to what we can accomplish! I became a successful businessman. And I'm thankful to God for that. But each and every one of us has to crawl out of that black hole, because there is a top somewhere. Any one of us can become a prime minister or a president or whatever. Every one of us has that chance, and so let's not stay in the black hole. We have to get up, not to be on the couch! Climb up, climb, *climb*! God will help us all to do that."

A silence, an appreciation, a dream filled up the austere room in the far suburbs of San Diego. Latino sadness, Jewish pain, and Christian poignancy mixed into the room of musty air and stirred hearts. Lou murmured an additional prayer out loud, asking each of these kids before him to "take an inch one day, then another inch the second day" in the direction of just loving other human beings.

One of the teachers spoke up about the then-recent massacre of little children at Sandy Hook Elementary School in Newtown, Connecticut.[10] She told Lou and the students about something the parents of the victims were doing—creating simple "acts of kindness," one after the other, in order to heal and improve the world that we live in.

"Yes, that's what we have to do," said Lou, gazing at the young people with a look of unconditional love and inspired purpose. "One good thing and then another, that's what we have to do."

The session ended in applause and tears. As he does at every visit to every school, Lou Dunst invited the youngsters to come up and exchange hugs with him. It happened to be during the week of his 87th birthday. The teachers presented a cake, the students sang "Happy Birthday," and the survivor blew out the candles.

A corresponding little wind blew through the leaves of the blooming trees near Auschwitz in Poland and the meadows adjacent to Mauthausen in Austria. Above, six million angels closed their eyes in devotion, knowing that they somehow remain beloved.

---

10   In 2001, a multiple shooting occurred in Santee, California, a suburb of San Diego. Lou was called to the site in the aftermath and reassured both students and teachers with his wisdom and narrative.

CHAPTER NINE

"My Name is Israel"

LOU DUNST IS RARELY SEEN EITHER WITHOUT OR NEAR A PRAYER
book. He is not judgmental about what prayer book it is—that is, from
which Jewish denomination it was published. He prays and studies in
three congregations in San Diego: Reform, Conservative, and Orthodox. He
does not adjust his religious attire, regardless of which synagogue he is visiting:
there is always the colorful little yarmulke on his head and a *tallit* (prayer shawl)
around his shoulders. He leafs through the siddur (prayer book) in his hand,
or the *Chumash* (The Torah; Five Books of Moses) with a veneration that is
laden with absolute and pure adoration for both God and the Hebrew liturgy.

His weekly Sabbath ritual on Saturday mornings generally happens at a
downtown Conservative *shul* known as Ohr Shalom ["A Light of Peace"]. Sitting
and standing next to him during a religious service is an emotional experience—
not because he brings any special drama to it, but because he is wrapped in
more than his *tallit*. He is wrapped in the right to deny and denounce every
possible reference in the book to godliness, beneficence, faith, and forgiveness.
Yet all of that is as far from his heart as it could possibly be. He actually has no
argument with God. His soul is pure in its devotion and gratitude to *"Ha-Shem."*

When Lou is called to the lectern for an occasional honor during the service,
such as blessing the Torah scroll in the course of its weekly reading, some people
in the congregation stand up quietly. He does not particularly acknowledge this.
He is too focused upon his own devotion to the liturgy and is a bit withdrawn
with divine distraction. So there is this silent dynamic of honoring his life and
his burdens that is not lost on this sweet old Jewish man, but is not conceded
by him as necessary or even that vital to the overall community celebration in
the synagogue. Lou has a number, 68122, that is burned into his soul but the
numerical value of his ego is zero.

I asked him once: "So did you pray in the camps?"

His answer: "We did whatever we could when it came to that."

But when we sat together in the synagogue, both holding the *Art Scroll Siddur*,
a handsomely presented prayer book from traditional sources, he pointed out

something inscribed therein that gave him direction and purpose—even when he could not grasp a holy book of any kind in that most unholy of places, a death camp.

"Now look," said Lou, turning the pages of the book with typical reverence and care. We were sitting in a business office for this interchange but he naturally wore his little kippah atop his head, which still reveals a good sheaf of white hair.

"Okay," he says, intent, leafing through the book of devotions, psalms, and theological poetry. "Now we know that my [Hebrew] name is Israel. It starts with the [Hebrew] letter *yud* and ends with the letter *lamed*. Okay." Lou puts his finger on a specific word on a particular page of the book; the word in Hebrew is 'ISRAEL.'

"And this is my name," he announces with quiet pride. The survivor is eyeing a special section in the back of the book that makes creative relevance of people's Hebrew names by connecting names (Rachel, Jacob, Sarah, David) to scriptural verses. *Yisroel*, or Israel, the hallowed register indicates, is inscribed within Psalm 118, because a key fragment of the piece begins with the letter *yud* and concludes with the letter *lamed*.

לְאָרְשִׁי [Yisroel]

"Now," continues Lou, "when we *daven* (pray) the *Amidah* (the Standing, usually known as *Shmone Esrei*—the Eighteen Blessing's' Prayer), we come to this exact phrase that begins with yud and ends with lamed, which is the beginning and end of 'Israel.' Well, this is my name, Israel! And what does it actually say here?"

Lou is excited and emphatic, almost in epiphany.

"The phrase says, 'Let me live, so I can tell the doings of the Lord!' Okay, so I changed it a little bit and the way I say it, the way I believe it, is 'Let me live, so I can tell the story!' This was my bargaining with God. If He let me live, I would tell the story, the happenings of God. So that's it. That's my name, and that's what I am doing."

Lou's friend, Alberto was with us when he explained this to me, turning the pages of his beloved devotional, putting his fingers gingerly on God's names and verse, earnestly clarifying to me his deepest convictions and sense of obligation. So there were the three of us in the room, an austere conference area in an office suite, suddenly filled with divine sparks. One could only recall the time-honored dictum of Talmud: "When three sit together and study Torah, the Divine Presence rests among them."

....

When Lou talks about Mauthausen and his subsequent, razor-close succumbing to death at Ebensee, what follows is a dissertation brimming with residual bitterness, unfathomable complication, and psychological victory. His descriptions are at once harrowing and inspirational—a trip to, and over, the pit of despair and dissolution taken by a person whose anguish and faith will never run out. Yet the two, anguish and faith, make a bed in Lou's soul: you see this in his calm eyes and his broad grin.

Still, the story comes out of him with a sure sense of purpose—a tone that is informative but edged with resolve: that the listener should know.

He repeats: "In Mauthausen, we were like zombies. We cried for just some water, maybe a piece of bread, anything. They told us not to worry; we were going to the gas chambers anyway. Sure enough, in the morning, we were all gathered, we were naked. We were pushed out on the steps and forced down to the building. The building is still there. This was the gas chamber. Down we go, into the building. Doors open from the inside, we are pushed in. We look around, and nothing is happening. There was not enough air to breathe. Some people are falling down, they are fainting because they could not breathe. We are terrified and holding onto each other."

Then a miracle occurred—one of several incidents that Lou resolutely pronounces as divine interventions. In Auschwitz, the gas did not rain upon him and the others because of a mechanical failure or just some inexplicable twist of fate. Now, in Mauthausen, according to Lou, God was again laying celestial fingers upon his head.

"All of a sudden, the doors open up and they are screaming at us, 'Everybody out in a hurry!' We are told to run to the *appellplatz*[11]—this is the center part of the camp where most of the important things were done. We were still naked there. And we were put into groups of 68,000, 70,000, and 72,000. My brother Irving and I wound up in the group of 68,000. He was right behind me. Like always, he made sure that he was taking care of me. He put his hands on me whenever he could. He always wanted to be sure where I am. So off we go and we were numbered."

As Lou has explained, he and Irving were never tattooed for the simple reason that they were twice immediately scheduled for asphyxiation in the chamber. Why should the Nazis waste the ink? Now, instead, "We were numbered with a bracelet. My number was 68122 and his was 68123."[12]

---

11   *Appellplatz* is a compound German word meaning "roll call" (*Appell*) and "area" or "place" (*Platz*). The word is generally used to describe the location for the daily roll calls in the concentration camps.

12   In fact, though Irving's bracelet, #68123 was lost, Lou donated his, #68122, to the National Holocaust Museum in a public ceremony. "Google me and you will see it!" he proudly announces.

Why were Lou and Irving spared the gas a second time, that horrific day in Mauthausen? Why did he wear—and keep for all time —the bracelet made from the discarded cans of Zyklon B pesticide instead of just perishing in the gas chamber? The answer comes from Lou himself, as he recalls the commandant of Mauthausen and what that individual actually said out loud that day of "the miracle."

"He made a statement," narrates Lou. "He said that to burn our bodies was too expensive. Instead, he would send us to a place where we would vanish without any cost to the Third Reich. And that's exactly what he did."

That place was Ebensee.

Ebensee, one of about forty sub-camps of Mauthausen, and regarded by many prisoners and historians as the most savage and merciless of these kinds of work-to-death centers, was created because the Nazis wanted to make rockets—as we shall see.

PHOTO TAKEN BY SERGEANT ROBERT PERSINGR'S BRIGADE SHORTLY AFTER ARRIVAL
AT EBENSEE CONCENTRATION CAMP, MAY 6, 1945

In 1998, the Austrian Resistance Archives published a booklet about the sub-camp written by Florian Freund. The 63-page documentation, cold, meticulous, and terrifying, was translated into English by Max Garcia. Garcia, a survivor of this place, was the inmate referenced in Chapter One of this book who enticed Persinger, the GI tank sergeant to come down from the armored vehicle when he noticed the soldier lighting a Lucky Strike. "It's been a long time since I had a Lucky Strike," boldly declared the emaciated Garcia on the liberation day of May 6, 1945, as he looked up at the filled-out serviceman in military attire poised safe and high above the landscape of contaminated and lifeless people.

That little breakthrough of interaction and smokes would lead directly that day to the recovery of inmate 68122, Lou Israel Dunst, who was within moments of his last breath atop a heap of corpses.

Why did Ebensee and similar "starvation camps" (as they are described by some chroniclers) come into existence? In fact, the impetus for this place was the basic failure of initial Nazi war policy. The "Blitzkrieg" strategy of overwhelming and destroying the enemy's military power by merciless surprise attacks and unceasing bombardment did not totally succeed—except in Poland. The Germans had planned to quickly obliterate their enemies, and then exploit the occupied territories. When that approach fell short, they decided to expand the concentration camp system—all to support the Nazi economic and working needs. Bondage labor, mostly Jewish, would be pressed into the manufacture of munitions, armaments, and a vast assortment of industrial needs. As Lou expounds: "They took everything from us for themselves. They took our homes, businesses, and bank accounts. They turned us into their sub human slaves. They turned our ashes into fertilizer, our skin into gloves and lamp shades, and our hair into all kinds of domestic products, done by Ilse Koch,"

As one German historian has written: "The aims of the concentration camp work were not only production and profit but also the destruction of the producers and the elimination of those who did not belong to the 'ethnic community' of the Germans."

The SS, while being above all a genocidal syndicate, was the dark bureaucracy and the criminal administration that was ultimately charged with providing "units" (human persons) to the industrial and production centers that were the death camps. The SS had its own companies and affiliates; they were making money wielding power on the crumbling backs of the eleven million Jews of Europe who were the lowest on their racial totem pole. The assessed death of six million of these eleven million Jews—from France to Poland to Denmark to Greece—remains an estimate.

Ebensee was known as *Projeckt Zement* ("Project Cement")—a sub-camp that nonetheless had an explicit mission to fulfill: the development of rocket technology and manufacturing. Lou often mentions that the renowned but controversial rocket scientist Wernher von Braun was on the scene at Ebensee.[13] Other such camps focused on the Nazi chemical industry, aircraft construction, electro-technical efforts, and the building of tanks and more conventional missiles. Ebensee was about the "wonder weapon" that the Nazi propaganda machine claimed it was creating—a super rocket that the Allies deeply feared and wished to eliminate before it gave the flagging Nazi war campaign a sudden, even apocalyptic advantage that could completely rewrite history.

But Lou and Irving Dunst had little awareness of these large and dangerous implications for the world. They just knew that, as horrifying as Mauthausen had been, and even with the miracle of again being spared the gas chamber, this place Ebensee was unimaginably macabre.

Says Lou: "The commandant at Mauthausen had made it clear, that we were being sent to a place where we would simply vanish without any cost to the Third Reich. This was what Ebensee was all about. We were marched to the railroads and into the boxcars and this was my fourth trip in the boxcars. But there were only men, mostly young men. No more children, women, or old men. They were all gone by now. Off we go. Last stop: Ebensee! One of forty sub-camps of Mauthausen. *FOR-TY,*" Lou emphasizes, raising his hand as if to enumerate.

"This was no kindergarten. It was one big colossal organization of killing. The conditions there for us were absolutely horrible. Starvation. They worked us day and night. We were doing underground work, in tunnels, in the mountains, to build missiles to go to Washington, DC, and New York City." At this point in his presentation, Lou mentions that Wernher von Braun—"He was the top man of the missiles"—was there from time to time, "to supervise. And after the war, he was the top man in the United States for the missiles!"

Lou tells of an endless, desolate, terminal cycle of work and torment. "The underground place that I worked in was three stories high, a full-size railroad

---

13   According to records published by the National Aeronautics and Space Administration (NASA), von Braun developed the potentially war-altering V-2 rocket for the Nazis but later turned his allegiance and brilliance to the United States. Dr. von Braun became director of NASA's Marshall Space Flight Center and the chief architect of the Saturn V launch vehicle, the super booster that would propel Americans to the Moon.

station. It was a big operation—big. They worked us day and night, with beatings, torture. A lot of it was mental torture. The commander of the camp would round up inmates and have his dogs trained to tear the flesh off the bodies of people. We were told this is what happens to people who don't obey. He would take inmates, chase them into the bushes, and do hunting and killing for pleasure. This is what happens to people, they told us, who try to escape. I don't think he was human, that commander. He was a beast."

Lou pauses; the memory of that time and place stops his spirit for a moment. "Our conditions…." His voice trails off. "The bottoms of my feet were frostbitten and swollen. But we still had to go to work, no matter what, in the freezing stone quarry. We worked in the stone quarry at night and in the day we built the camp. They would not let us sleep. From one job to another job. Starvation was beyond description. Most of us, including myself—we had hardly any flesh left on us. No muscles on our bones. We couldn't stand up. We couldn't walk and that included me."

Thousands of these living dead, the *Muselmänner*, were soon piled atop each other near the crematoria. Many were dead, none—including Lou—had anything resembling life in them.

One of the Holocaust memorial sites within Germany offers a published exposition about the ghastly phenomenon of the concentration camp, the *Muselmänner:*

> The term *Muselmann* was used in the camp language to designate prisoners who were so emaciated by hunger, cold, disease, and exhaustion that they became unresponsive to their surroundings; all that remained was an interest in obtaining food, at times also protection against cold…. The quantitative and qualitative malnourishment, excessive physical labor, harmful effect of the clothing and unsanitary living condition were factors that helped turn a prisoner into a *Muselmann*. The *Muselmänner* suffered from emaciation and lost their ability to work; their posture became stiff and stooped and they shuffled along, taking tiny, shaky steps; and because of their physical frailty, they often fell and injured themselves. They ceased to be concerned with personal hygiene and lapsed into a state of neglect, wearing filthy rags, and they suffered from purulent infections and open sores all over their

bodies. The even more wretched appearance of the *Muselmänner,* with their fear-filled or expressionless eyes in gray, puffy faces, set them apart from the mass of the prisoners. Only their eyes said something now and then, they still could react. These were men to whom fate had been unkindest, the most unfortunate of all the unfortunates.[14]

In Ebensee itself, as in other similar horror camps, people began to lose their minds—especially when it came to their searing hunger. Survivors of Ebensee reported incidents of prisoners literally licking spilled soup (the watery, unsavory rotten beets soup barely edible to begin with) off the grimy floors. When caught doing this, they were beaten out of their senses by guards. One eyewitness account reads as follows:

> The prisoners ate everything that they could chew: leaves, grass, and even pieces of coal. I still remember when they brought a load of a soft type of coals into the camp for heating. The consumptive and despairing prisoners spoke about the possibility that inside these coals there were certain fats, that margarine could be made out of, and they began to eat the coals. A large number of prisoners died because of that.[15]

Lou Dunst closed his eyes in pain, sorrow, and despair one night in Ebensee. He had spoken to the despondent Russian officer whom he noticed sitting by himself for a moment in the camp, asking if this older person could make sense of the situation. He had received the answer, from the center of a hollowed-out soul—that the man's brain was made dysfunctional by the reality around him. Lou shut his eyes, quivering with the hunger, the cold, the terror. He recalled his childhood home back in Jasina, briefly, painfully. He could hear in his mind the news of the outside world—usually not so good for the Jewish people—that came through, mixed with static and danger, from the only town's little radio tuned to the BBC. When would the outside world ever come to rescue him and Irving and all the miserable, hopeless people left to disappear in this living hell that seemed forsaken by *Ha-Shem*?

---

14   The Norbert Wollheim Memorial, Frankfurt
15   From Florian Freund's Concentration Camp Ebensee

It was the spring of 1945 and the prisoners knew that a decisive moment was nearing. It was discernible in the body language of the Germans, the undercurrent of rumors and sometimes more credible reports that filtered through into the camp, and even in the sudden, panicked bursts of new levels of bestial treatment on the part of the guards and *kapos*: the Allies were nearing. If Lou could hold on, if he could cling to life; if Irving could continue to grasp Lou's shoulders when they had the rare chances to intersect, then maybe the liberation would come. And then Lou could begin to fulfill the letters of his name and begin to tell the story.

It was approximately two o'clock in the afternoon, Sunday, May 6, 1945. The camp commander, Anton Ganz, had already made his sinister speech, instructing all of the inmates to gather in the tunnels "for their safety." Eyewitnesses would report later that Ganz had grown increasingly unpredictable, anxiety-ridden, and fitful in the previous few days. In fact, he and all the resident SS officers had fled the camp by the time the strange and wondrous rumblings of Lady Luck and the other US Army armored vehicles were heard. Staff Sgt. Robert Persinger was about to see things he's still remembering now, seventy years later. His tank breached the fences of Ebensee and, by 2:45, the camp was liberated and Irving Dunst was dragging a GI along through the pyramids of corpses to find and free his brother Lou.

....

"Israel shall be your name. For you have struggled
with the divine and with men, and you have prevailed"
[Genesis 32:29].

TOP: LADY LUCK AND ITS CREW WAS PART OF THE CONTINGENT
OF THE THIRD CAVALRY OF GEORGE S. PATTON'S THIRD ARMY.

BELOW LEFT: AFTER CAPTURING THE GERMAN FLAG.

BELOW RIGHT: EBENSEE RAILROAD TRACKS USED TO BRING THE
PRISONERS TO THE EXTERMINATION CAMP IN THE INFAMOUS BOXCARS.
(PHOTOS FROM ROBERT PERSINGER'S BRIGADE MAY, 1945)

CHAPTER TEN

"How would I have behaved?"

T'S NOT HARD TO BE AROUND LOU DUNST. THE AURA OF "A SURVIVOR" wears off, though it never dissolves completely. Except when he is addressing groups and telling his story (for which he only accepts charitable donations for causes related to life and education), he doesn't speak about death camps, brutality, and sadism. He talks about you, your family, your health, and all the blessings he wishes upon you. He enjoys a good meal with friends at his favored San Diego delicatessen; he is always treating everyone else, admonishing them to study the menu and just enjoy, and holding the door open for the other person as all enter or depart.

Lou spoke with me on a drive we shared beside the Southern California coast. His deep, healing eyes gazed along the shimmering shoreline and he said: "What a blessing to be alive and to live in this country!" He is not given to small talk—not because he is aloof or dismissive. It's just that he values every opportunity to speak, to tell, to listen, learn, and teach. Every word is a consecration and a privilege to a man who was meant to be silenced before he even became a man.

We began to talk about the Torah. Somehow, the topic of the biblical character "Yitro" (Jethro) came up. Jethro was the father-in-law to Moses even though the elder was the High Priest of Midian. The entire Torah portion that contains the Ten Commandments is named for this pagan, Jethro.

"I know all about it!" Lou practically shrieked with delight. "That was my Bar Mitzvah portion!" This was the Bar Mitzvah ceremony whose timing was dictated by the imminence of the Nazis—scheduled two months earlier than the calendar dictated.

A lively and heartfelt discussion ensued in the car as we pointed out to each other how inclusive the Torah is—naming the Ten Commandments section for a non-Jew simply because he was a good man who guided and helped Moses. "Of course, why not?" exclaimed Lou. "We are all brothers and sisters! The tradition is for everyone. We share this earth."

Then Lou pointed out, with a delicious sense of irony, that not a single portion of the Torah is named for Moses. "But Noah, not a Jew, has one named for him.

And he was righteous but 'only in his own time.' The Torah is wise in this way. People are only as great or not great as the times they live in." One is struck by this aphorism spoken by a man who has seen and suffered the absolute worst behavior in human annals.

Lou continues to talk about the Torah. "And then there's one portion named for Balak, a foreign king who sent Balaam to curse our people. Such a great thing, that the Torah lets anyone get a place in history. And Moses, he was so humble, that not a single section is named for him. Oh, the Torah is so wonderful! I study the portion each week I learn something new from the material each and every time."

Lou chortles with scriptural love and with his ardor for the loving God he gleefully calls *Ha-Shem*. Then he remembers a little story from his youth about grain.

"Once I had a field of grain. It was back in the Sudetenland. There was a lot of grain so things were good. Then I realized there were rats. Very disturbing, the rats liked the grain. I went to another gentleman nearby who also had grain and asked him, how do you get rid of the rats? He told me that I had rats because of the grain, that's how it works. 'You can't get rid of the rats. They are there because you have grain. Better you should have the grain in the first place.' Naturally, I thanked him for his wisdom."

Lou's politeness and courtesy are both constant and instinctive. He does not know how to be harsh. Every molecule of the Nazi insanity, its bestiality, its savage and encrypted lack of regard for humanity, its feasting upon pillage, rape, bondage, and murder, are not lost on this gentleman. Every time Lou picks up a fresh, clean glass of water to drink, or hugs a child, or shares an idea with his characteristic squeaky delight, he defeats the Third Reich. It is not unlikely that, in his lifetime, Lou Dunst will have answered the Holocaust with six million acts of kindness.

And Lou has a sharp and lively sense of humor. This disarms some people who expect a survivor to remain eternally somber, grave, angry, or even suicidal. (There have been far too many who indeed took on some or all of these characteristics; no one who was not actually there can possibly imagine what psychological abysses they are trapped in, nor judge them). But, from faith to funniness, Lou chooses life.

I asked Lou one afternoon, after he had just completed a particularly lively and evocative appearance before an adult community service group, "How do people get a hold of you, Lou? When they want you to speak or meet with them?" Indefatigable, upbeat, even after the two hours of speaking and answering questions, the 87 year-old survivor cheerfully piped up: "They just call me! I'm in the phone book."

"They just look up 'Lou Dunst?'"

"Sure!" He retorted, his face turning into a mischievous smile. His eyes twinkled with glee. Then he added, enjoying himself thoroughly: "Sometimes, it's a problem. The name Dunst, I mean. Somebody called one day and said 'I'd like to speak with Kirsten Dunst.'"

Kirsten Dunst is a relatively well-known, quite attractive young American movie actress. Without skipping a beat, Lou reported that he immediately announced to his caller: "So would I!"

His close friends and family help Lou catalog the hundreds and hundreds of handwritten letters he receives from the people he addresses. They thank him, praise him, and bless him. The school children, in particular, express their admiration and awe and respect for his candor and his courage. He especially enjoys recalling one note that arrived in the mail from a high school girl who listened to him one day and found herself inexpressibly moved.

"She said to me, 'Mr. Dunst, I love you so much that when I get old enough, I'd like to marry you.' I wrote her back and said, 'That's wonderful, but my wife might have a problem with it!'"

His grin is at least as big as his pain. Yet he clearly believes that he is entitled to laugh, tease, and cajole—exactly because of what the Nazis put him through.

Lou doesn't ever delve deeply into his understanding or analysis of the Nazis. He just states what happens. There are occasional flashes of indignation but he has, by choice or just instinct, rechanneled such impulses into declarations of his belief in the State of Israel, or—more frequently—his avowal of "the unity of the family." There are always touches of his family history, what his father taught him, how his mother loved him, how his brother held on to him. But investigative psychology of the Nazis is nil. It's their horrifying obsessions and their grueling limitations as human beings that matter to Lou. He doesn't study them; he survived them.

And yet: there is a clinical evaluation of the Nazis (and their innumerable citizen collaborators of every European nationality) that can be derived from Lou's declarative style. He says about them: "There is nothing that they wanted or desired that they could not get. They just took it from us. This was something that has never happened before or ever since in history."

Historians, chroniclers, anthropologists—none have stated it more clearly. What Lou and the other millions suffered was the consequence of one thing: appetite. It was appetite of the most diabolical form, even as it was founded upon the starvation of others. When we apply the term "appetite" here, we are not talking about simple hunger. We are talking about the greatest outbreak of dark avarice in history. When we talk about Lou and all the other Jews being hungry, we are not talking about that they were waiting for their next meal. They were starving to death.

The craving that the Nazis had for Jewish blood, treasure, property, and sexual gratification was easily fulfilled. It was enjoyed without limitations. "The free world did nothing about it," Lou laments. He does resent the indisputable facts that the Allies knew about the shooting squads, the deportations, the camps, the genocides, the unspeakable violence that was so methodically structured.

One could break into the familiar arguments that the Allies had their hands full trying to stop the greatest armament and arsenal of destruction ever created and that defeating the Axis was the way to stop the killing of the Jews. This viewpoint is lost upon Lou. Like all the others, Lou was not part of a military map. He was a living corpse buried in a continental cemetery.

Nor is Lou influenced by any heroic applications some would make of the Jewish disaster in Europe. I mentioned to Lou on one occasion that some assert the following: the genocide of the Jews was actually a decisive factor in the defeat of the Third Reich. If the Nazis, they argue, were not so busy and distracted by the industrial murder machine required to kill so many people as quickly as possible (and the annoying problem of having to dispose of so many bodies); if they did not have to assign so many officers, engineers, technicians, scientists, supervisors, to the task; if they did not have to divert so many railway systems, materials, power lines, sewage systems, and infrastructure in general to erecting the fiefdoms of death—did this not all make a critical difference in their proportionately deferred power and thereby hand the Allies a gruesome advantage in the war?

"I don't really see it that way," responded Lou, soberly. "You know, they used us as slave labor. They had everything done and built for them without paying a cent for it. They simply used us. And not just us. They used the Russian prisoners-of-war, whom they treated almost as badly as the Jews. They had all kinds of groups of people. They got whatever they wanted, whenever they wanted. And when they were done using us to build and produce whatever it was they wanted or needed, they just killed us off and replaced us with more slave labor. So I don't think they lost the war because they were killing us. They actually had an advantage because they had us for slaves."

I was persuaded by Lou's take on this. In fact, Lou believes that it was the Russians who broke the back of the Third Reich—or, specifically, Hitler's misguided belief that he could attack Russia with impunity.

"When he sent his army into Stalingrad, he made a big mistake. It was the kind of mistake that comes from the arrogance he had and that they all just followed. They were absolutely sure that this new order of theirs would last forever. He underestimated the will of the Russian people when he went into the Soviet territory. They, the Russians, lost many, many people but they defeated him and that was really the end of it for him."

In fact, of the 59 million people who died during the Second World War, 20 million were Russians.

The Nazi command wanted to take Stalingrad for more than their coveting of the oil fields in the Caucasus region between the Black and Caspian Seas. It was Adolf Hitler's personal hatred for Josef Stalin that fueled his irrational obsession with the city named for the Soviet dictator. Conversely, Stalin made the question of saving Stalingrad a morale issue for his people and his troops. Two terrible men playing military chess with their satanic egos, mixed in with stifling cold and unbearable topographic conditions, sent millions of men and women to their deaths.

But Hitler truly lost the war in this vain effort; the German army was literally frozen and starved and went into retreat. Both sides had relatively equal numbers of troops, armaments, and planes. The Russians had the particularly rigid winter of 1942–43 — which the Germans did not anticipate nor were able to endure.

Nagyszőlős is a town of Russian descent named after the vineyards above it on the south side of Black Mountain. It is likely that this "village of grapes" lost many of its sons who perished among the Soviet soldiers trapped at Stalingrad. One of its sons, a Jew named Edward Hoffman, wound up in a strange and morbidly parallel path with Lou Dunst.

Nagyszőlős was about forty miles from Lou's birth village of Jasina, also flanked by the Carpathians. It sits on the banks of the Tisza River—which originates in Lou's hometown of Jasina. Lou and Edward, who is better known by his friends by the nickname "Boomie," met each other for the first time in 2013 in Southern California, some seventy years after their corresponding journeys from youth in the Carpathians to horror in the concentration camps. They both were rounded up, ghettoized, lost their parents in Auschwitz, endured successive terrors in the boxcars, and both finished in Ebensee. (Boomie arrived there from Dachau). They were both liberated on the afternoon of May 6, 1945, just after Sgt. Robert Persinger breached the fences and Lady Luck groaned through the sea of dead and dying.

Due to the circumstances of my knowing both men, though separately, I had the honor of arranging their get-together. When they encountered each other under sunny Pacific skies on a warm June day, Boomie, the heavier and cheekier one of the two, embraced the more formal Lou. I stood by and choked back tears. For some reason, the verse from Ecclesiastes rang in my mind: "All the rivers run to the sea."

Their own emotions were somewhat forcefully restrained as they distilled them in a series of greetings, blessings, and knowing intuitions via a medley of Ukrainian, Hungarian, Russian, and Yiddish expressions. Warmth, pain, and insight filled the space between them, which narrowed quickly along the path of raw memories. They shook hands first, then partially embraced—two men who in some ways reluctant to rub their wounds against each other.

"What barrack were you in at Ebensee?" Lou asked Boomie.

"I was in Barrack 27," said Boomie.

"I was in 6 and in 18," Lou informed him.

It was almost as if two nice old Jewish men were having a reunion of some disowned Boy Scout troop from a murky time and place too unbearable to explain to any outsider.

They both remembered that as soon as one walked into Ebensee, one encountered the decidedly plusher, canine-protected SS barracks. Then the "housing" for inmates unfolded, row after row of infernal buildings racked and ridden by suffering, lice, howling, and savagery.

"I had a *kapo*," said Boomie, "who was a professional killer. He built a hanging tree outside the building, just where you walked into the barrack. And he had a big bucket of water there. If he didn't like you, he pulled you out and pushed your head into the water until you are dead. I got to Ebensee in March [1945]. A lot of people died...."

I remarked to Lou: "You saw these kinds of things all the time, I'm sure?"

"Some of it," Lou responded politely. Then, falling back into his good nature, he teased Boomie about being a "greenhorn" at Ebensee, since the latter arrived within two months of the May 6 liberation. Lou endured the place considerably longer although, Boomie, dumped there from Dachau, was no greenhorn in the category of suffering. The two men treated each other with respect and insight and they shared the kindred spirits of interminably scarred psyches.

Lou said: "You know that Ebensee is the only one that I know of that historians say had a special hospital for the Jews. Did you know that? It was called 'Revere.' For the Jewish people it was a special one: A one-way street."

Boomie nodded in grim agreement. "Nobody came out," he said.

"One way! One way!" Lou exclaimed.

Then Boomie spoke again: "The last two months before liberation, I had to—they put me to take some of the bodies from the crematorium. I'm looking and I see: some of the bodies had the *tuchases* (buttocks) cut out." Lou nodded vigorously and knowingly. He knew where Boomie was going with this account.

"They used to cook those parts to eat," reported Boomie.

"Yeah, sure!" Lou chimed in, for the author's benefit. "Cannibalism. It was widespread, like I've told you." The two survivors chuckled together, the kind of guttural, collaborative laugh that signaled their brotherhood and their shared desire to teach an American from the postwar world what really happened just seventy years ago.

Lou questioned Boomie: "Did you have any Jewish *kapos* in your barrack, too?"

"Yes." This was so evidently a very sensitive issue and topic for the two men, just as it was for the millions of living and dead in that netherworld. "I had one, he was Jewish-Polish."

"Was he okay?"

"Well, he couldn't be okay. How could he? He had to kill people in order to survive himself."

Then Lou drew a breath and spoke to both of us: "You know, sometimes I question myself. How would I have behaved if they would pick me to be a *kapo*? Of course, I was too small, I was a little nothing. But I'm trying to figure it out. Who knows? Who knows what people become when they have to make such choices?"

"Who knows?" Boomie grunted, his thick, sad eyes blinking under his rimmed glasses.

The men talked again of the days before the Nazis came down the Tisza River.

Lou and Boomie referred to Nagyszőlős by its Yiddish name: שילעס (Seylish). Like Lou, Boomie attended *cheyder*, wrapped phylacteries around his left arm every morning with the Hebrew prayers, prepared for a bar mitzvah ceremony, and was constantly and maliciously surveilled and accosted by young fascists and anti-Semites.

Boomie's family had significant portions of land and they owned mills and oil fields. His family also included furriers and, somewhere along the line, he took up baking—which served him well as a craft when he made it to the United States after the war. Both men, defying the very writ of Nazi ideology, have succeeded and prospered as businessmen in this country.

Lou, of course, came from a warmly-knitted family unit, sharing space and holidays and religiosity in the house that doubled as a general store. There was some jostling at the table between the two of them: Boomie boasted of his children's achievements. "One of my sons is a federal judge!"

Lou has no children. He questioned Boomie: "Do you speak at places like I do? You know, I tell the story sometimes three, even four times a week, to high school kids, businessmen, Navy Seals."

"Well, no, not really. I've been asked a couple of times. People are always curious, you understand that. It's not so much my thing to speak about it in public."

The two men, once little boys with quiet dreams in the Czech/Hungarian fields, sat and sipped coffee in a Panini restaurant in California. People chatted, studied menus, and checked their email on smartphones.

They men smiled at each other in warm anguish. In the end, Boomie was #42117 and Lou was #68122. In both their cases, their numbers were grafted onto bracelets made from the discarded Zyklon B pesticide cans.

But the numbers remain tattooed into the souls of two nice Jewish men who are trying to live normal lives after surviving the most abnormal times in human history.

EDWARD HOFFMAN AND LOU DUNST.
LAGUNA WOODS, CALIFORNIA, JUNE 2013

CHAPTER ELEVEN

The Sisters of Mercy

LOU DUNST DOES NOT RECALL WHERE OR EVEN IF HE SLEPT DURING the night of Sunday, May 6, 1945. The rest of the world may have "clocked" that liberation day at Ebensee, hour by hour, from approximately 2:45 PM on through the first forgiving evening and night of freedom for the inmates of *Projekt Zement.*

But for Lou and Irving Dunst, those hours were a blur—a hazy distortion of inconceivable news, hearsay, hope, confusion, elation, and upheaval. To this day, Lou cannot specifically recall the sequence of events that immediately followed the thrust of "Lady Luck's" tank muzzle through the fence and the deliverance of the camp. Soldiers in boots were running, many in shock; GI rations were being practically thrown at barefoot, cadaverous, limping bodies; kapos were being hacked to death by vengeful prisoners; men in uniforms were retching; emancipated inmates were literally blowing up from ravenously scarfing down foodstuff that their shrunken, juiceless, polluted stomachs were fatally rejecting. The clamor of freedom cries, qualified by the last powerful crescendo of death, hung in the stinking air like the din of reckoning day.

And yet: out of this reckoning would come another day. Says Lou: "Even the atheists started praying to God."

The report prepared by Florian Freund about Concentration Camp Ebensee contains the following description:

> With the camp liberated, chaos broke out. For at least one day nothing worked in the camp, water and electricity failed, and masses of prisoners stormed the kitchen and the bakery. Many liberated prisoners went into the village of Ebensee in order to look for food with whatever means at their disposal.
>
> The unnatural and quick eating had catastrophic consequences for many of the half-starved prisoners: suddenly a number of different illnesses began to appear which caused the death of many of these weakened prisoners after the liberation."[16]

---

16   From *Concentration Camp Ebensee: Subcamp of Mauthausen.*

"I really don't remember too much about the first day, the second day," says Lou. "I was nearly dead. Somehow, my brother located me and got me into the army hospital that they set up. They didn't have anything to work with. They did their best. Irving and I both fell into their care. They worked so hard. But they hadn't known that they were going to discover the camp that day and at that time. They knew they were near camps like this. But they didn't know that May 6 was going to be the day. So it was a very confused at first and people were still dying all over the place."

Freund continued his narrative of the indistinguishable first two days and nights following the jubilation:

> On May 8, the Americans took measures to save the prisoners' lives. UNRAA [United Nations Relief and Rehabilitation Administration] Team 122 and the 30th American Field Hospital, later on also the 139th Evacuation Hospital, arrived in Ebensee. It was truly a great effort of both these mobile American hospital units who had only a capacity to take care of 800 patients to deal with of thousands of patients from one day to another.
>
> When the 30th Field Hospital arrived early on May 8, there was no clothing, no housing, no food or eating utensils, etc., yet in a very short time they were successful in reducing the daily death rate immeasurably. In the systematic examinations of the prisoners they found out that the average weight of the prisoners was 39.09 kg (76.7 lbs.)....
>
> ...At least 735 prisoners died after the liberation, most of them because of weakness in the body.[17]

There was no organized convoy or route or working mission to help Lou and Irving out of the liberated, if crippled camp back to their home. There were as many possible ways home as there were survivors; it was hardly an organized effort driven by the Europeans who had participated in, or acceded to, the slaughter of the Jews. Lou and Irving were on their own when it came to returning to Jasina. Edward "Boomie" Hoffman, mentioned in the prior chapter, was a little bit luckier. He happened to become one of the young people collected to safety via Great Britain's *Kindertransport*—also known as

---

17   Numbers substantiated by the 139th Evacuation Hospital records.

the Refugee Children Movement (RCM). After a brief period in nearby Linz, Austria, he was mercifully airlifted to London and spent several transitional years in foster care on a farm north of Dublin.

Boomie's case was exceptional. Lou and Irving, orphaned by the genocide, not even aware that strangers lived in the Dunst home (and still do to this day), were left to their own wits. "There is not one single Jew left in my town," Lou emphasizes. He has visited his former town several times but the house with the general store long ago passed into non-Jewish hands.

Other refugees did drag themselves across long journeys, in still dangerous and hostile provinces (the Nazis surrendered their troops, not their hatreds) to former homes in places such as Gdansk, Kiev, Lyon, Krakow, Budapest, Gargždai, and Viški—to mention just a few. When Jews returned to reclaim their dwellings, they were often beaten up or just killed. There were still sporadic anti-Jewish pogroms in Poland as late as 1946 and 1947.

The Allied armies could generally do little. They had the millions of prisoners-of-war to house and feed and process; they had the entire process of demilitarization and occupation and judicial complexities that now came with rebuilding the continent that had destroyed itself along with 59 million lives. They were certainly aware of the Jews but they did not prioritize the Jewish relocation back to their homes.

Nor, in the vast majority of cases, did the Jews have homes anymore. It wasn't always a case of the house being destroyed by bombs or fire or just vandalism. It was frequently a matter of the home now being occupied by someone else—an individual or family righteously acquiring the house as part of the Nazi policy of *Judenrein*. The survivors of Ebensee, Mauthausen, Auschwitz, Dachau, Treblinka, Bergen-Belsen, and so many thousands of other camps and satellite camps were liberated. But that hardly meant that they were free.

It is important to Lou that people understand the anarchic nature of the Jewish world in the immediate aftermath of the cessation of hostilities between Germany and the Allies. "Most of the killing stopped. But that did not mean that we just got up, walked away, and went back to our lives. We did not have our lives, ever again."

Lou remembers about "graffiti." After a brief stay at a military hospital ("They didn't have anything to help us with, but they did their best"), they set out together. They trudged along beaten paths, occasionally hitched short rides in the horse-drawn wagons of more sympathetic wayfarers, and snuck onto the tops of freight trains. They were refugees—homeless, stateless, ultimately nameless. Along the way, scrawled on walls, fences, makeshift signs, and on handheld billboards they saw the graffiti of the lost Jewish world, in a variety of languages:

> Have you seen my son? Yossele, 16 years old, brown hair, walks with a limp?
> My mother may be alive. Papa killed. But Mama is missing. Esther Devorah.
> My husband was a minesweeper for them near Lodz …
> Uncle Avram is 44 but they liked him for work…
> My cousin Shimon …
> My wife …

"This graffiti was usually found at the soup stops and the free kitchens they put up here and there," said Lou, referring to this somewhat unusual phenomenon of kindness that sprouted up along the burnt paths of the postwar landscape. "We were trying to orient ourselves. One way we did this was to write graffiti on the walls. We gathered in those places where there was a bowl of soup, something to eat. We were hungry. We would write on the walls, like others did, 'My name is so-and-so and I'm going home to Prague, to Berlin, to whatever it was. And we are looking for this one or that one.' We were looking for someone who was related to us. Any information. Anything that could help us get our bearings or just some news. We wanted to connect. But we couldn't find anything. Everybody was lost and everybody was a stranger. Nobody knew who they were looking for. One comes from here, one comes from there. One was liberated from this camp, one was liberated from that camp. We didn't find people that we knew. But this is what we used for some kind of little support system."

Lou and Irving had no need to post any graffiti about their parents. There was no question that both of them were gone, murdered at Auschwitz-Birkenau. Cremated and vaporized; ashes floating somewhere between heaven and earth. But their sister, Risi: could she possibly be alive? They scrawled her name on some of graffiti walls but did not carry much hope she could be found or had survived the dreaded camp.

"Let's try to get to Bratislava," Irving said to Lou.

Bratislava is the capital of Slovakia; although the government had deported some 15,000 Jews into Nazi hands, the brothers still had relatives there. Irving had attended a *yeshiva* (Talmudic academy) in the city, which fell to the Russians by the end of the war. In the whirlwind of their post-Ebensee existence, it just seemed like a logical destination. But it would hardly be an easy one.

The problem was that they had no cash, no food, and their physical circumstances were frail and feeble. They were infested with ailments, contamination, dysentery, and lice. They were unwanted and vulnerable. It didn't take long for them to realize that they were in need of some kind of medical intervention and that they were not going to get to Bratislava immediately. Lou's feet were still crippled by the frostbite that set in during the Ebensee internment. He says: "Most of the time, I just kept thinking that *Ha-Shem* was testing me." He warmed his soul by remembering the sweet butter in his mother's kitchen that she used to prepare the warm bread twice a week, "once for the regular days and, of course, the challah for Shabbos."

The road led through Linz and then on to Prague, where Lou and Irving wound up in the Podoli Sanatorium. Today the facility is known as the Institute for the Care of Mother and Child and it operates in immense premises along the Vltava riverbank. Dedicated doctors had created the clinic just before the outbreak of the First World War; it was founded as the "Pražské sanatorium" [Prague Sanatorium]. In the First World War, part of the sanatorium was transferred to the Red Cross and became a military hospital. By the time Lou and Irving were admitted there after their liberation from Ebensee, it was a hollow shell of itself, battered and broken by warfare, terribly lacking in supplies.

After their brief stay in Podoli, the brothers planned to part. They acknowledged that they each had to pursue personal destinies but promised to eventually reunite—in Israel. Lou puts it characteristically: "My brother went one way and I went another way." But they first trekked—usually as castaway hobos—on the top of railroad cars. "We didn't have any money for the fare," says Lou. "We had nothing. No papers, no supplies." They would make their last jaunt together to Bratislava.

In that city, Lou, so terribly weak from typhoid, stayed behind while Irving ventured to a house where relatives of the Dunst family were known to have lived. "Then came another miracle," recounts Lou. Irving knocked on the door and it was opened by their sister, Risi.

Risi was not the same, however. She had survived, but she had not lived. "She was depressed for the rest of her life," Lou says quietly. "The camp changed her." Risi, the oldest child of Mordecai and Priva Dunst, was twenty-three when the war ended. Lou is uncommonly reticent when the subject of his sister is put forth.

One can only imagine a once-vibrant girl, the apple of her parents' eyes, with a sweet, if shy personality living life in the crisp air of the Carpathian Mountains. Now a permanent shadow was evident in her face and the things she had seen and experienced in the horror were too large and too intense and too evil for her to even speak about. Even those who survived were all stricken, from one degree to another, by the silence of death.

Risi was not completely defeated by the camp experience; she married a man named David Adler and they had a child together. They were eventually able to arrive in the United States and make a life for themselves. But the torment, the weight of her grief for her parents, the entrapment in hell at the vicious hands of mass murderers, left her marked physically and spiritually. Lou is not given to reveal details about his sister—even if he has them. His long face and lowered eyes tell us more than any testimony. Rather than offer any specifics about "the miracle," Lou politely summarizes the event as something he never expected. "We didn't know. We knew nothing. We didn't know what to expect. We were never oriented. We didn't know where we are going or what we are doing. Mentally, we were so depressed, so drained from everything."

Somehow, listening to Lou, I felt that he was presenting me with a metaphor for his forlorn sister and that was the best he could do.

In Bratislava, even as Irving was putting together his plans to join with a Zionist group and head for Israel, Lou all but succumbed to his typhoid fever. "I was checked into the Catholic hospital," he says. "It's still there," he adds—always an advocate for things and people to endure. Among the Sisters of Mercy, whom he praises and thanks in his heart for their post denominational care and compassion, Lou regained a modicum of strength.

Lou has simply never forgotten the benevolence and diligence of those nuns. "They had nothing to work with, nothing to give us. No medicines, really. But they were so kind and did whatever they could." Then, with his trademark twinkle of the eye he narrates the following:

"There were no pills, no drugs, nothing. They comforted us with their hearts. One day, a sister gave me something to drink. 'What is it?' I asked her. 'Cognac,' she replied." Lou giggles a bit while recalling this. "She said, 'Drink it. And if it feels good to you, I'll give you another!'"

Fifty years later, Lou returned to the Catholic clinic. "I went there to personally thank them for saving my life," he tells every group that he addresses.

He then stresses his abiding theme that "we are all sisters and brothers and we are all God's children."

Lou's unrelenting philosophy of universal brotherhood not only transcends the murderous culture of the Holocaust, it supersedes the pitiful predicament of the postwar Jews who found themselves still alive. Here are some historical facts:

> After the collapse of the Third Reich, Europe was in a smoking shambles. The smell of death filled the air across the continent. Hundreds of thousands of people were homeless and seeking a new life. In general, they were referred to as "displaced persons" or more typically as "DP's." They had nowhere to alight and were largely despised. In dealing with these wretched people, the European community did not exactly have a reservoir of moral tradition to draw from in the wake of what had just happened.

Among the DP's, which included the two Dunst brothers, were several hundred thousand Jews who had either survived the horrors of the concentration camps or escaped the Nazis altogether. The United Nations was created in 1945, in the war's wake. Resettling these displaced persons was the specific responsibility of the United Nations Relief and Rehabilitation Administration (UNRRA). Like so many UN bureaucracies to this day, UNRAA was stricken with incompetence or skewed by the deeply ingrained biases, especially anti-Semitic biases, which still pervade in the UN.

In 1947, because of difficulties with the UNRRA, a new organization, the International Refugee Organization (IRO) took over the work of finding homes for the displaced persons.

In fairness, resettling the survivors was a daunting task. When the IRO took over in 1947, there were still about 1,200,000 Jewish and non-Jewish people looking for homes. In the next four years the IRO did manage to relocate about a million people.

The Jews represented a serious and special challenge for the IRO. Nobody wanted them and they themselves often carried mixed feelings about returning home. Home was where the majority of them were first plucked viciously from quiet and innocent existences and thrown into the maelstrom. Like Lou and Irving, so many knew that their parents and other relatives had been murdered; what was the meaning of their former houses and streets and schools and synagogues when it was certain that these places and their prior warm-blooded inhabitants had all been destroyed? Where, in this smoldering inferno called Europe, was the meaning of the word "home?"

So a lot of the Jews lacked the desire to return to their villages. We have noted that some Jews were, in fact, murdered by mobs when they tried to return to Poland. In a 2006 review of a book about this dark spectacle, *The New York Times* reported:

> One might have thought that if anything could have cured Poland of its anti-Semitism, it was World War II. Polish Jews and Christians were bonded, as never before, by unimaginable suffering at the hands of a common foe. One might also have thought there'd have been pity for the Jewish survivors, most of whom had lost nearly everything: their homes, their youth, their hope, their entire families. Besides, there were so few of them left to hate: only 200,000 or so in a population of 20 million.
>
> Instead, returning Polish Jews encountered an anti-Semitism of terrible fury and brutality. Small wonder, then, that nearly as soon as they set foot on Polish soil, most fled all over again. Many went westward, to a place that, oddly enough, had suddenly become an oasis of tranquility and safety by comparison: Germany. Far from being celebrated, those Poles who had sheltered Jews during the war—and there were many—begged them to say nothing, lest their neighbors deride them as "Jew lovers," or beat them, or break into their homes (searching for the money the Jews had surely left behind) or kill them.[18]

The most notorious postwar pogrom[19] took place in the Polish town of Kielce, which had been ethnically cleansed by the Nazis. Forty Jews were killed in cold blood by townspeople on July 4, 1946. The incident was spurred by a false report of a child kidnapping and was essentially a savage example of the ancient practice of a blood libel against Jews. The mob violence was proven to have been instigated by members of the Soviet-dominated Polish Communist Party.

---

18   From David Margolick's review *of FEAR: Anti-Semitism in Poland After Auschwitz. An Essay in Historical Interpretation,* by Jan T. Gross.

19   Pogrom is a Russian word meaning "to wreak havoc, to demolish violently."

COFFINS OF JEWISH VICTIMS OF THE 1946 KIELCE POGROM THAT
TOOK ABOUT FORTY LIVES. [THE *NEW YORK TIMES*]

Only about 200,000 Polish Jews were even still alive in 1945—the country had been a world center of Jewish cultural and spiritual life for centuries that once contained three million Jews. The Kielce travesty convinced survivors that not even the tiny Polish remnant had much of a future in this former national capital of *yiddishkeit*.

Lou Dunst was grateful for the cognac and compassion given to him by the nuns in their modest church hospital. But he was restless for something that he knew inside of himself had disappeared along with his parents—a safe haven, a destination, a home. Irving was already dreaming dreams of heading for the land of Israel, known then as the British Mandate of Palestine. Even though the British were hostile towards Jewish emigration to their spiritual home, and even blockaded and imprisoned Jewish DP's who tried to reach the shores of Haifa and Tel Aviv, Irving felt what many Jews knew: Israel was the only spot on earth where they might finally live in peace and safety.

The dye was cast. Risi was alive. Lou would slowly recover from his ailments and he talked things over with his brother—who had kept his hands on Lou's shoulders in the subterranean realms of the Nazis and who now sought the light of the Promised Land. The brothers hoped to eventually reunite in the new Jewish state and they made some provisions and plans to do so in time. In a parable of biblical pathos that summarizes the desperate plight of countless survivors of the Nazi Holocaust whose lives were irreparably altered by the genocide, Lou repeated: "He went one way and I went another."

They would be emotionally inseparable till Irving's death in 2012. But their geographic trajectories were beginning to diverge nonetheless, at least for a while.

The Angel
By Jenna Soensksen

I walk into the room,
expecting an old man to be waiting,
but the creature before me is not a man,
but an angel.
An angel sent by the Lord
to preach his story
of how he was handpicked by God
to endure and suffer in childhood,
to look Death in the very eye,
and to pull away
by His faithful agent disguise in Army green.
The creature before me,
radiates in the brilliance of hope,
spreads his golden wings,
and speaks directly to the soul.
The angel before me speaks of peace and harmony,
of tranquility and kindness.
The angel before me has lived a thousand years,
spreading his story has become his humble duty
He has flown all over,
opening the eyes of thousands just like me,
renewing faith, showering us in wisdom.
The angel before me
is Mr. Lou Dunst.

CHAPTER TWELVE

"Rome was a crossroads"

I N THE SPRING OF 2013, LOU DUNST RECEIVED A HANDWRITTEN NOTE— one of thousands he has received from people who have heard him tell his story in the United States and other countries. This one was penned by the program chair of a women's service group in Southern California:

> *Dear Lou,*
> *The ladies all agreed that you were the best speaker we ever had! You have a light within you that shines and can never be extinguished. Keep up your message. The world should never forget the Holocaust.*

The letters flow in after every presentation. Hardened combat veterans reveal their teary understanding of what Lou describes; they also suffered from isolation and fear and imminent danger during warfare against the Axis, in Korea, and Vietnam. But they discern that the experiences of Lou and the other millions of Nazi victims surpass all terrors. And they were soldiers with guns and air cover and provisions and strategies.

A Hispanic high school boy, writes to Lou and declares, "You are my brother." Lou's lectures, always culminating in emotional question-and-answer sessions, are often hosted or blessed by rabbis, ministers, and priests. On the opposite page is a poem written by a high school student inspired by one of Lou's talks.

Respect for other faiths is at the center of Lou's personal protocol even while he draws deeply from his private source and faith—Judaism. He recalls a moment he shared with his wife Estelle while they were visiting the Vatican, decades after the war. (Lou and Estelle have travelled the globe in search of Jewish life and in order to share Lou's narrative of hope.)

"People were lined up to visit the statue of Jesus. It's a magnificent setting and I honor it. They were all Christians, good pilgrims, and they kissed the feet of Jesus when they came up. I chose not to—but only because it's not my religion! One of the guards came over to me—he was not angry—but he simply asked, 'Why did you not kiss the feet of Our Lord?' I responded, 'I mean no disrespect at all.' The man knew that I was sincere. I told him, 'I respect the Catholic faith but I just happen to be Jewish.' He understood and everything was okay."

Lou is no stranger to Rome, meanwhile. He first arrived there, rolling in like tumbleweed from Prague, in 1947. The Italians had begun the Second World War II in tandem with Hitler and under the frenzied dictatorship of Benito Mussolini. "Il Duce" was deposed in July, 1943 and eventually publicly hung, famously upside side down, in 1945. Reversing themselves, the Italians concluded the war fighting alongside the Allies. The Rome into which Lou arrived, alone and penniless, was something, in his words, "of a crossroads in Europe for people trying to connect to somewhere else and maybe rebuild their lives."

A three-minute vintage film with both black-and-white and color imagery, entitled *"Rome: The Eternal City,"* was produced by Walton Films in 1947. Something of a silent Christian travelogue, it reveals a postwar city that is bustling with automobiles, pilgrims, markets, churches, and white-clad traffic policemen directing commuters from atop plaza stations with spinning ivory gloves and almost ballet-like motions. The film is anchored along Via dei Fori Imperali, which "runs through the heart of ancient Rome."

It may very well be that the Jewish and penniless survivor Lou Dunst arrived in Rome that year entering via the new "postwar railway station." It was adjacent to the Arch of Constantine. Not likely that he toured the various, timeless attractions that were open and bustling—as though there hadn't just been a war and a concentric circle of genocides. Lou may have quietly walked past the stout Franciscan monks in dark robes and tethered belts; he might have made his way through the Piazza Venezia, where huge crowds had once hailed Mussolini; he may have looked for room and board as he passed by the Basilica di Santa Maria Maggiore—dedicated to the Virgin Mary.

Lou did not casually or even accidentally visit the Coliseum, the Forum, or the Spanish Steps. Nor did he stand and observe the Swiss Guard in their regalia protecting the grand portals of the Vatican. Lou Dunst was a speck in the imperial glare of Rome—a hungry, scrawny, refugee Jew left to his own recourse under the indifferent domes and arches of St. Peter's Square.

Lou was lonely, deeply so. For the immediate time Irving was detained in Cyprus by the British, was determined to get to Palestine—and the nascent state of Israel where Risi and her family were already there. Though the brothers had distinct plans to reunite in the new Jewish state, this would depend upon a number of factors and could not be assumed. Lou was alone though resolute. He thought of the uncommonly angelic nuns that had helped him recover from typhoid. Their mercy and dedication ("They worked day and night and though they didn't have medications, they gave us their hearts") offered him strength and a renewed faith in humankind.

Trudging along in Rome, he remembered the afternoon in the Catholic clinic when he and a couple of other Jewish patients began to tease their nurse/sisters. "We told them that we were making a bet: were they brunettes or blondes under their veils?" Lou chuckled to himself in the middle of the eternal Christian city. "They laughed and told us that we seemed to be getting better and that was what counted."

Then Lou thought about his brother. "Irving went to something called *Hakhshara*" (Hebrew for "preparation"). He was among this group of people that, after the war, were going to what was then Palestine under the British Mandate. In November of 1947, the United Nations Security Council responded to Britain's desire to quit its colony and the blistering civil war there between Jews and Arabs. The Council passed the Palestine Partition Resolution by a vote of 33–13, which divided the territory into two states (something never realized when the Arab nations invaded the Jewish section and were defeated in Israel's Independence War of 1948–49).

The Partition Resolution represented the only instance in history when the United States and the Soviet Union voted together in favor of any resolution. International guilt over the genocide of the Jews pervaded and drove the vote for a renewal of the Jewish homeland and the ingathering of the exiles.

"Irving was more of a practical man than me," Lou explained. "He was stronger, a man who worked with his hands, not so much an intellectual. That's why he did better in the camps than me. They used his skills as a wood worker, an engineer. He wanted to go to Israel and be free. He was a Zionist."

The *Hakhshara* were agricultural institutes similar to *kibbutzim* (communal settlements) where young Zionists were able to learn or sharpen technical skills necessary for their emigration to Israel. They were indoctrinated with the socialist principles of the kibbutz movement. The challenge—even before they would get to the land—was to overcome the treacherous journeys by foot, over mountains or across seas, or the increasingly brutal British naval blockade of the leaky ships that would transport the Jewish DP's from Europe to the Palestinian shores.

The British, who frequently detained the refugees in harsh holding camps on the island of Cyprus, had basically chosen the Arabs over the Jews in the Palestine conflict due to traditional British industrial and economic ties with Arab oil interests. "They were also just plain anti-Semites," Lou says bluntly.

"Well, I wound up in Rome and my brother wound up with the group trying to get to Israel," Lou summarizes. "They bought a ship but it was not seaworthy. The British picked them up right on Israeli shores. They took them to Cyprus.[20] Irving was there for about a year. He couldn't go until the Jewish state was established.[21] They were mistreated by the British. Irving told me that they even had these kinds of long swords that they plunged into his backpack to see if there was something in there. They just cut off the straps. They were very anti-Jewish."

Seattle-born Elihu Bergman, an energy specialist who participated in the dangerous "illegal immigration" of Holocaust survivors and fought against the British blockade that stopped Irving Dunst and so many other Jews, wrote an essay entitled "*Facing the British Blockade with Rusty Ships.*" Bergman, who died in 2005, was one of several hundred North American volunteers who risked life and limb trying to counter the inhumane, even sinister determination of Great Britain to stop Jews who were unwanted, stateless, and desperate from reaching the one place on earth where they were welcome:

> In a virtually unknown episode after World War II, a small group of American and Canadian sailors participated in an operation that transported Holocaust survivors to Palestine. At the time, Palestine still was under British rule, and the British government continued a pre-war policy that limited Jewish immigration to several hundred persons a month, with the ultimate objective of barring it entirely. So a rescue operation was mounted by the Palestine Jewish underground, and conducted under clandestine conditions. It was called "illegal immigration."
>
> All told, a fleet of 68 ramshackle ships transported more than 73,000 "illegal immigrants" from European ports between 1946 and 1948. Among them were 10 American ships, acquired as war

---

20   This was a typical practice of the British during the period and many former death camp inmates were prevented from reaching Israel—a heartbreaking outcome. Thousands were imprisoned in poorly-erected camps on Cyprus.

21   Israel was declared independent and the British formally departed on May 14, 1948, setting the stage for a massive land invasion by five Arab armies.

surplus from U.S. bone yards and crewed by 240 volunteer sailors and contract officers. The 10 American ships carried 31,000 would-be immigrants, or 43 percent of all immigrants to Palestine in that period of time....

Only a handful of ships — not one U.S. vessel — penetrated the British air and sea blockade deployed to prevent any arrivals in Palestine. The blockade, backed up by an assortment of economic and diplomatic obstacles, extended from the Palestine coast through the Mediterranean, to the chancelleries of Western and Eastern Europe, and even to the U.S.

Upon reaching the Palestine Coast, the ships were routinely apprehended by the Royal Navy. With one exception, their passengers were transported to prison camps in Palestine or Cyprus. The exception was the *Exodus 1947*, an American ship, whose passengers were returned first to France, where they refused to disembark, and then to Germany, where they were forced off the ship. Earlier, when the *Exodus 1947* attempted to make landfall in Palestine, marines from a British warship boarded the ship. In the process, the marines clubbed to death Bill Bernstein of San Francisco, the second mate of the *Exodus 1947*. Numerous American and Canadian crewmen of the *Aliyah Bet* ships were interned in Palestine or Cyprus, along with the Displaced Persons they were attempting to bring into Palestine.[22]

While Irving was being detained and then languished behind barbed wire and bayonets on Cyprus, Lou began the long process of putting together some kind of meager life in Rome.

I asked Lou, "So how long were you in Rome?"

"A year, a year and a half. "

"And what did you do in Rome to sustain yourself?"

Lou described his first living arrangement: he slept in the hallway of a tenement house, while garnering various odd jobs during the day in order to cover the rental fee for this begrudged space. His entire existence was wrapped into a blanket that contained all his meager belongings and sense of self. Lou always

---

22   *'Facing the British Blockade with Rusty Ships,'* essay by Elihu Bergman, on web site of Aliyah Bet & Machal Virtual Museum.

paid his debts back to those who showed him even the remotest kindness in the years after the war: "I told many people that if I couldn't pay them now, I would return and pay them later. Or I would do anything, absolutely anything, to take care of my debts. I'd sweep the floors, clean the toilets, whatever it took. And I did. And if I still could not pay, I returned later and paid. I did this every time and for every person."

Soon enough, Lou upgraded to an actual room, "with other Jewish fellows there. We rented part of the apartment that a woman occupied, the lady of the house. She had two children, grown already. We slept there."

"These were all Jews?"

"All Polish Jews. Most of them were receiving money from relatives in the United States. This is how it was for many people. Everybody was just trying to start over in situations they could not have imagined. We all lived day to day, just trying to keep a little bit of money in our pockets."

But Lou, a survivor of four death camps and of circumstances that remain incomprehensible even to him, did not settle for a "day-to-day" existence. Slowly, tentatively, but resolutely, he began to reconfigure his life and his own security.

"Then I started to be a middleman," he said. "People came from all over, many of them for business. Rome was a crossroads. Some of them were even coming from Israel. They needed to trade money to make things happen. And I would be the middleman: if one had dollars, and the other one had *liras*[23] (the Italian pound currency until 2002), I'd put you two guys together and make the trade and earn some commission. Didn't matter what—sometimes it was gold against *liras* and *liras* against gold, dollars against something else. Whatever."

So there in Rome, Lou developed a money exchange business. "I did very well. I started with commissions from someone else and then I did it on my own. Then I bought a BMW convertible."

I interjected: "You did very well!"

"Not a new one!" Lou smiled and clarified. "They didn't have new ones yet. This was a pre-war made vehicle." Lou explained that he sent the car off to Israel, to his brother Irving; they were still planning and hoping to reunite there and start a significant production enterprise.

"And I also bought some machinery," he added. "This was for wood work or furniture manufacturing. My brother and I had been planning that I would eventually also get to Israel to work together and make furniture."

---

23   In fact, the correct plural form of the Italian lira is "lire."

Lou reminded me that when he and Irving were kicked out of their school as kids back in Jasina, they were assigned to a woodworking group. The fascist plan was to always put the Jews into a situation where they could work—before their eventual extermination. "Irving and I were sent someplace where we were taught something to do with our hands. It was a special school. He stuck to it and I didn't. I was a business mind type of guy. But we helped each other with everything."

The two emaciated survivors of Ebensee had this dream—to combine Irving's strong mechanical skills and Lou's powerful business instincts into a new and prosperous life in a free Jewish state. Only part of the strategy was realized: Irving did make it to Israel and worked in various plants, "in factories for building busses and other such things," and Irving made a decent living. But the brothers were not destined to reunite in Israel. "None of it materialized," said Lou. "It did not happen."

LOU AND ESTELLE IN FRONT OF BURNT TORAH.

CHAPTER THIRTEEN

"We can pray anywhere!"

L OU HAD THE OLD BMW CONVERTIBLE, THE INDUSTRIAL EQUIPMENT, and the dreams—all slated to land in Israel. Then a call came from Israel: it was his brother-in-law David, married to Risi. The car had actually been purchased for David and Risi to use in Israel even as the family planned to reunite there with Irving and develop a manufacturing business.

"There was a change in plans, suddenly," said Lou. "A switch—there were always switches and changes in those days. Things were never certain. David told me not to ship anything. He was coming to Rome. But it was too late, everything was already shipped."

David sent a letter to Lou telling him not to travel to Israel; he was coming to Rome. Things hadn't worked out so well for him without *"zitsfleisch."*[24]

It was 1949. David finally arrived in Rome. "And then he and I—by that time I had some kind of papers to travel to Canada—so he and I went to Canada," said Lou. "And then we brought his wife and child over as well."

The Dunst story of family members planning, retreating, gleaning government travel papers, re-strategizing, separating from one another temporarily, and then (if they were lucky) reuniting somewhere, was but a microcosm of the breathtaking, often desperate narrative of Jewish survivors following the end of the Holocaust. No group, no society, and no nation particularly welcomed them and no community especially reached out to them. They had survived, only to scramble.

I remarked to Lou: "No matter what the circumstances, when David arrived in Rome, it must have been wonderful to see him."

Again, that strange silence whenever a potentially emotionally moment occurs for to Lou. There is no question that he loved his brother—it's clear that when Irving died in 2012, Lou grieved profoundly and that, in a sense, something died within him. He is clear-eyed and direct with his refrains about Irving and himself: "My brother saved my life during the Holocaust. If he were here now, he would say that I saved his life. We never lost sight of each other and we carried on the family unity that saved both of us."

---

24 The Yiddish term is explained a few paragraphs below.

And yet: there is this notable reticence—a curtailing of sentiment when it comes to the recalled moments of safe passage, reunion, or just emotion itself. I first observed this when Lou detailed the return home to Jasina of his beaten and savaged father from the minesweeping responsibility for which the Nazis had brutally enslaved him. The family had not known when or even if Mordecai would reappear. When he did, they simply did not have the time or the strength to rejoice. Rejoicing comes when people can relax and savor the end of a struggle. When Mordecai emerged alive from the kidnapping and the incarceration, they were surely relieved. But it was all they could do not to simply dig in and prepare for the next atrocity.

Speaking once to a group of Catholic college students, Lou quietly declared: "There are wounds that will not heal." Lou is open about almost everything and he readily invites questions at his lecture engagements. He is a bright window to a dark chronicle and he exhorts his listeners, with smiles and teases, to inquire, to learn, and to be affected. "Nothing is off limits!" He frequently affirms.

But it's not altogether true, though Lou is not given to secrets or mysteries. There just are some things he keeps to himself and people seem to know that these categories are beyond his curriculum. These are "the wounds that will not heal" and even Lou Dunst is unable to express them. He just tells the story to the best of his ability and without disturbing the subterranean layers of his soul where it's too painful to go.

Life for the Jewish people after 1933 was not linear; it was not a series of milestones nor was it even written or spoken in sentences that ended with periods. Life was—and to some degree still remains—a series of weak and uncertain commas. Such a language does not even have a vocabulary for sighs and reprieves. One just looks up, acknowledges a development, and then looks down to gird one's loins for the next misfortune. Not only did Jewish people die; Jewish souls passed on.

So Lou speaks about his cherished brother-in-law in a matter-of-fact fashion: "He was not an educated man. But a good tradesman, you know, good at what he was doing. He didn't have what they call *zitsfleisch* in Yiddish. He couldn't find himself. So he brought over his wife and his little girl. But that *zitsfleisch*—it means, literally, 'he can't stay put; the flesh, the meat doesn't sit, one is restless.' So then he decided to take his family from Canada to the United States. And they did. And I remained in Toronto."

nbered "a lady there by the name of Mrs. Jacobs. I'm still in touch with her daughter. I stayed with them in Toronto. They were very nice to me. I had room and board. I think I paid thirteen dollars a week. She made lunch for me. I got a job, though it was very hard to find work. Remember—I wasn't trained for anything. So I finally got a job in the needle trade."

Toronto, now a twenty-first century world-class cosmopolitan city, was just emerging into its glistening future of skyscrapers, lakefront towers, and international banks. Its subway was being dug, and even though the central Jewish community of synagogues and delicatessens along Spedina and Bathurst Streets was evolving, the beaches along Lake Ontario were still infested with signs reading "No Dogs or Jews Allowed."[25]

Lou had a bit of a problem with his status in Canada not long after his arrival. His right to remain in the country was actually questioned because he had no paperwork or certification that he was a citizen of any other country. It was a gratuitous, even cruel twist even if it was a bureaucratic reflex. How was a person who was driven from his home, had his parents murdered, thrust about the killing fields of Europe by the Nazi regime, stripped of any national status, supposed to be able to verify a citizenship that had been pitilessly stripped of him? "I was a refugee, a stateless person, whatever you want to call it, all those names. Except being a citizen or belonging to some country. I was just a Jew."

The problem was solved in yet another brilliantly improvised move by Lou. "I stood and declared, 'I hereby formally renounce my citizenship in my former country!'" And the Canadian authorities acquiesced and allowed Lou to attain landed immigrant status. "That did it. They were relaxed. They didn't have to feel guilty giving me a piece of paper, a visa, telling me that I fit in there."

But Lou was soon enough planning to immigrate to the United States (he now had the proper documentation). He wished to rejoin his brother Irving as well as Risi and her husband, David Adler, and their own child. Through all the spirals and surprises, the aspirations for a life in Israel, America emerged as everyone's destination. Risi, still plagued with the depression that never left her for the rest of her life, was settled in Los Angeles with the family. David was established in small-scale manufacturing. In those days, extended kinfolk were still a clan; the hallmark value espoused by Lou, "the unity of the family" was much more than just a phrase.

---

25   It should be noted that after the war, and in the wake of the genocide, the Canadian government actively legislated a variety of anti-discrimination laws; the Jewish population of Toronto grew from about 60,000 in the mid-1950s to over 150,000 now.

"My aim was to go to Los Angeles," said Lou, "but I wanted to stop by and see my aunt—my mother's sister, Sarah." The aunt lived in New York. "Just to meet her and say 'hello,'" added Lou. The diversion would bring with it many new twists.

....

It was actually a little more than a question of wanting to "stop by and say hello" for the modest Lou. Certainly Lou carried a natural desire to see the sister of his murdered mother, Priva. It would have been inconceivable for the young man to exit Canada and head straight for California without taking the opportunity to visit with an elder so biologically connected to one of his lost parents. But Sarah's son, Lou's cousin, carried a deeply personal saga that affirmed Lou's longstanding avowal of "the importance of family unity."

The young woman named Helen, raised in New York while Lou, Irving, and Risi were living as small children in Jasina, was an accomplished student with a special acumen for medicine. She aspired to become a physician—not necessarily an open path for a female, especially a Jewish girl in the earlier part of the 20th century and even in the United States. She was turned down because, as Lou relates, "there were already too many Jewish medical students." Indeed, the quotas placed on Jewish students by American medical schools are a matter of record.

Mordecai and Priva Dunst arranged and paid for their niece's transfer to Vienna, where she was able to enroll and study to become a doctor. "My parents supported her," Lou said, matter-of-factly. (Just a few years later, in 1938, when Austria was annexed by Nazi Germany via the *Anschluss*, Adolf Eichmann arrived in Vienna and personally managed the decertification, incarceration, or murder of Austria's Jewish physicians. 153 of the 197 professors at the University of Vienna Medical School were Jewish; they were removed, sent to concentration camps, or committed suicide.) Lou's cousin was able to complete her degree and return to the United States by 1938 and established a practice. Now, when Lou arrived to see his aunt, he found only the doctor—Aunt Sarah was on extended visit in Florida, visiting a son.

Lou shut his eyes in a mixture of fatigue and frustration. As always, a flutter of throbbing memories filled his head. He thought of the entrapped Jewish forging specialists, forced to use their printing and lithography skills by their Nazi tormentors in Ebensee: under threat of death, they created endless stacks of impeccable counterfeit money bills for the SS. The Nazis then used these in wide circulation.

He recalled the deeply loathsome usage of expert Jewish naval officers on Nazi submarines, pressed into service by the Germans because they were so accomplished—only to be murdered after they were no longer of use to the Third Reich. He thought, as he did constantly, of his mother and "I wanted to see my aunt, my mother's sister," he told me. So after one or two nights, Lou set out for Florida.

"Before I was going to get to Los Angeles," he repeated in his inimitable way, "I wanted to stop by in Florida, you know, just to say 'hello.' To give her a kiss."

Lou arrived in Miami Beach. "It was Byron Avenue! I don't remember the number, but it was Byron Avenue." His visit quickly evolved into an extended stay because of Aunt Sarah's son, a lady's wear manufacturer, convinced Lou to remain and take a job. "So I did. Miami Beach!" Lou laughed with affection and gratitude.

The postwar world was rumbling with industrialization and suburban expansion. Dwight D. Eisenhower, the supreme Allied commander who, white-knuckled but resolute, had postponed the D-Day invasion of Normandy by one day due to weather and then saved the free world in this maneuver, was in the White House. Unknown to most any being but God, Lou Dunst had somehow made his way from New York City to Miami.

Like a scrawny measure of Jewish tumbleweed, Lou had traversed the Pinelands of New Jersey and then through Philadelphia and onto the coast of Maryland through to Virginia Beach and Chesapeake Bay. America was vast, open, and free; Lou marveled at the casual intensity of the people, their unencumbered access to food, services, and to one another. He passed by Kitty Hawk, North Carolina, likely unaware that the Wright Brothers had first winged there fifty years prior in a rickety, three-axis flying machine. Then it was on to Charleston, Myrtle Beach, and Savannah as Lou took in the thick live oak forests and the emerging red soil of the Old Confederacy. Finally, he entered Florida near Jacksonville and continued his relentless trek down the Atlantic Coast, through Daytona Beach, past antebellum mansions and endless orange groves, to his extended family in Miami: a land of palm trees, lush hotels, crammed delicatessens, and clusters of synagogues.

The Jewish tradition is somewhat ambivalent about fate and life and who or what is in control of this existence. How could God have allowed the Holocaust; where was "*Ha-Shem*" while six million innocent human beings, including almost two million children, were slaughtered? For Lou, there is no issue and no controversy: "God was there, even in the boxcars," he insists. It is easy to believe that without Lou's unyielding faith in a merciful God, Lou would have lost all hope and been consumed by a loneliness and dread deeper than anything else imaginable.

Lou doesn't dwell too much on the questions; he gravitates towards answers. He answers hate with love, evil with good, division with reconciliation. He is truly quite unafraid; after what he has seen and experienced in his lifetime, what is there that could possibly scare him?

He was in his eighties already, established as an inspirational speaker and a matchless storyteller, when he found himself one afternoon with an audience of skinheads and fascists. One or two of the grossly tattooed, hateful audience members taunted Lou, mocking his story, denying the Holocaust, and denouncing the Jews. Lou, at risk, unprotected, stood his ground. There was greater strength in his truth than there was in their hate. The notion of physically harming the sweet, roundish little Jew, with his spectacles, wearing his knit yarmulke, was unthinkable even to those present who were inclined to violence.

"I am living proof that it happened!" Lou exclaimed in his occasional high pitch. His conviction and faith were too much for their cynicism; they could not be men, these modern fascists, if they attacked the peaceful messenger who unabashedly declared, as he always does, "We don't need to hurt each other. We need to love each other." The hecklers stopped sneering and backed down. One of them sought Lou out afterwards and denounced the skinhead movement, with Lou as his witness. It was neither the first nor the last time that individuals have laundered their souls and made new commitments in Lou's presence—to humanity, to Judaism, to charity, to forgiving someone an old grudge or endowing someone with fresh conciliation.

So what of the Nazi and European ambition to kill off the Jews and what of their shocking success at vaporizing six million people and innumerable future generations? How does one account for it in terms of belief in a greater being than ourselves?

Lou Dunst would not even take on the debate. God is not the cause of evil, he would say. God gave us life and we are responsible for harvesting it. When men and women run amuck and simply murder and destroy, the only thing we have is God. "I spoke to *Ha-Shem* all the time!" declares Lou, over and over again. "I said to him, I'm a teenager. What good would my ashes do?"

Through and with God, Lou heard his parents guiding him, sustaining him, nourishing his lonely soul through the darkness and the pain and starvation and the degradation. God made Lou's creaking back straight and his tattered heart whole.

"And I made my bargain with God," says Lou. "If You let me live, I will tell the story of what was done to us so that others will not do it again to any other people." This is the theme, the devotion, the anguish, and the redemption that Lou has carried with him around the globe—from the starving villages of Rwanda to the cemeteries of Germany to the stricken streets of Pakistan to the tatami-matted houses of Japan.

"It doesn't matter where we are," says the survivor. "We can pray anywhere. The line is open! The phone is never busy!" He laughs boisterously—a bellowing prayer of relief and earnestness.

There was never a question about God with Lou Dunst. The question has always been with humanity.

But how then does this God of Lou's allow the man to be nearly killed in a traffic accident in Lakeland, Florida?

LOU AT THE UNIVERSITY OF SAN DIEGO

CHAPTER FOURTEEN

Last Rites from a Catholic Priest

LOU NEVER SAW THE TRUCK BARRELING DIRECTLY TOWARDS HIM. He was driving an old Buick that he purchased for $425. He was on the road in his role as a traveling salesman—a position he had earned for himself as he made his hard way up the ladder of renewal and survival. "I would load up with samples and go up the east coast of Florida." In fact, the death camp survivor would often trek over to the west coast of the state and into distant points in Alabama and Georgia.

On the day of the accident, Lou was hit, head-on, by a farmer hurling along in his pick-up truck. Lou was traveling down a Polk Country two-lane highway, the clothing samples tucked on the back seat and in the trunk. He carried a letter of recommendation from his employer attesting to his credentials as a salesman. He was alone with his thoughts, his mind nonetheless focused as he gripped the steering wheel of his second-hand vehicle. "I lived in that car, pretty much," said Lou.

The gentle man who had survived the boxcars, the ghetto, Auschwitz-Birkenau, Mauthausen, and Ebensee was now being disentangled, semi-conscious, with broken bones and bleeding lacerations, from the shattered glass and bashed frames of the old car.

He doesn't remember very much about the collision but he does clearly recall his strange conversation with an earnest and sincere Catholic priest at the hospital in Lakeland. Lou was rushed there by ambulance and was presumed to be losing his life.

"Yes," he chuckled. "There he was, this nice priest, and he's telling me that he is going to give me 'the last rites.' He explained this to me. After he told me what he was doing, I said to him: 'Wait a minute! There are two things against our conversation, whatever we are doing here. Number one, I am not dying. Number two, I am Jewish.'"

As Lou recited this exchange, his smile lit up the room in which we sat with energy and light. Here was a man in total command of life and death—all of it managed with laughter and tenderness. "So," he concluded, "we had a nice conversation, this priest and me. I spoke to him with full respect, of course."

I queried Lou about his stay in the Lakeland hospital, curious as to how this survivor, with little means at the time, reimbursed the clinic for his stay and treatment.

"Well, I said to them that I had no money for what they were doing. But I told them that if they cured me and helped me get back on my feet, I will clean toilets, I will sweep the floors, but you will get paid. And they allowed it and eventually I came back and paid them."

Lou then added: "I afterwards decided to get off the road."

At the time of the accident, Lou was working for his nephew Yehuda—the son of his Aunt Sarah. "Yehuda—Joseph—called himself 'Joe' in America." Lou was planning to eventually head to California and reconnect with his David, his brother-in-law, but had to build up his resources and his experience before making the journey across the continent.

He was learning English—one of the several languages Lou Dunst speaks and understands with more precision than he concedes he does. He dialogues with people in English, German, Russian, Czech, Ukrainian, Yiddish, Hebrew, and several other dialects that are the product of his grim European saga. He laughs and cajoles and encourages people in all these parlances but with the singular language of loving kindness. He forgives the Florida truck driver, he embraces the Catholic priest, he calms the skinhead, he thanks the nuns that treated him with cognac, and he blesses the memory of his parents, brother and sister. He invites whomever he greets into a conversation of conciliation, immediately listening for and reverting to the instinctive language of his visitor. He holds the door open for anyone he's walking with, asks about his or her family, and he telephones a substantial list of friends and acquaintances every Friday afternoon—just to wish them "a good *Shabbos*."

Every single thing that the Nazis tried to twist or torture out of him, from his flesh to his soul, have remained intact and turned over in favor of everything that the Nazis despised: love, prayer, charity, and life itself. "What else can I do?" he asks. "I survived because *Ha-Shem* decided I should. So I have to give back everything *Ha-Shem* wants."

Lou thought about these values and principles as he showered adjacent to the small room he rented while working for his nephew Joe in Miami. His life at the time, an amalgam of creased road maps, brown-bagged sacks of food, and pressed clothing samples was not particularly exhilarating. But it was life -and that made it sacred. It required his hardest work and diligence and that was that.

He told Joe that he was going to California and Joe acquiesced with blessing and a fresh letter of recommendation. The note stated that Lou was worthy of any job he asked for and that he possessed complete integrity. Lou was grateful then and he remains grateful to this day.

Recovered and determined, Lou set out for the cross-country voyage to Los Angeles—and, in his words, "more miracles."

David, Lou's brother-in-law and Risi's husband, reached out to Lou. "He wanted me to come to Los Angeles and become part of his organization. All the things we had planned before, in Israel, did not work out. But other things would work out!"

Fortunately, the old Buick, though significantly damaged, remained like its driver—salvageable and working. "We got it fixed up," said Lou. "And I drove it to Los Angeles."

I remarked to Lou: "But you were alone, you had to do it by yourself!"

Lou skipped past my statement and declared: "Now here comes the man, the father of famous twins. His name was Yufe. I met him along the way. His twin sons were unusual. One became a Nazi and the other went to fight for Israel."

Yufe was a Jewish peddler with a broad romantic heart who had come via Trinidad from Romania. Lou and he found a good compatibility. It was in the days when people were more given to encountering each other in the open; it was still in the postwar period of nomadic happenstances.

"Yes, we found each other while we were both traveling. We happened to be in the same place and got along. So we shared the gasoline and made our way. Then my car broke down. It was somewhere in Texas. So Yufe says, 'I'm in a hurry. Take me to an airport. I have to get to California.' So I said to him, 'Well, I'll have to carry you because this car won't go one inch!' So, somehow, we fixed the car and I finally dropped him off in San Diego."

Resuming their cross-country saga, Yufe elaborated with Lou about his strange twin sons. The boys, Oskar and Jack, became celebrated enough that a documentary motion picture was made about them, aptly entitled *Oskar and Jack*.

Separated from his twin six months after their birth in Trinidad, Oskar was brought up Catholic in Germany and joined the Hitler Youth. Jack stayed behind in the Caribbean, was raised a Jew and lived for a time in Israel, spending a stint in the army and obviously fulfilling his Jewish heritage.[26]

---

26 The story is corroborated in "The Mysteries of Twins," featured in *The Washington Post*, January 11, 1998. The two men also participated in the "Minnesota Twins Study" in 1979.

In 1996, director Frauke Sandig released a joint German-British production about Yufe's twin sons. It turns out that Oskar and Jack were conceived during a shipboard relationship involving the father and a German Catholic woman. The couple was bound for a fresh life in the Caribbean, idealistically framed in unnationalistic concepts. They viewed the world beyond its geographic borders and religious divisions. Unfortunately, they separated shortly after the twins' birth in Trinidad in 1933.

When their parents split, the lives of the identical twins took radically different turns. Oskar returned to Germany with his mother and became caught up in the spirit of the Nazi era. Jack initially stayed in the Caribbean with his father who raised him as a modern Jew—not particularly observant but identifying deeply with Jewish history and culture. This steered Jack to Israel; there was ultimately nothing identical about the twins' view of the world.

Of all the people in the world, Oskar and Jack's dad was the one picked up by Lou Dunst on his way to California in his battered Buick. Lou made it to the west coast with his passenger and dropped Yufe off in San Diego.

Lou went on to Los Angeles to rejoin David, Risi, and the emerging family warehouse commerce. Disneyland was newly unveiled and the freeways were being developed and two New York baseball clubs, the Dodgers and the Giants, were relocated on the western frontier. None of this was of consequence to Lou—not a bit of the glitter and magic and sports realignment was in the field of his vision. He was focused only on connecting with his family. For Lou, the greater world was at best, insignificant; at worst, a dire threat.

"Here I'm walking along on the sidewalk in Los Angeles some time later," continued Lou, "and who do I see but Yufe? I met him and we said to each other, 'Hello! How are you, what are you doing?' The whole thing was unbelievable!"

Lou, though ensconced in Los Angeles with the family, was not really earning too much and he was actually looking for work on the day this astonishing new encounter took place. Yufe told his friend that he was working as a peddler in San Diego—why didn't Lou come down there and join forces with him?

"If you want to see what I'm doing," Yufe offered Lou, "come down and see for yourself."

Lou shared a somewhat uncomfortable report: In Los Angeles, he had gone from door-to-door, calling on wholesalers who might give him an opportunity to peddle their goods. "None of the Jewish owners helped me. They would not trust me. They would ask me for proof that I was good, for letters of recommendation, more than I had, for this and that."

So Lou jumped at the chance to try out San Diego with Yufe just as he considered the unanticipated reunion with him to be "another miracle!"

Elvis Presley played the San Diego Arena in the spring of 1956 but it was doubtful that Lou was aware of that—or even of Presley. The San Diego Freeway, connecting Los Angeles to the southern coast was being constructed. The expansive city that sat gracefully next to Mexico was nonetheless still a decidedly Navy town, a relaxed spread of sea vessels, Marine bases, and a modest skyline of hotel buildings. Here Lou came with high hopes and the extended hand of an unlikely sponsor that he had serendipitously picked up in his old Buick just a couple of years earlier. He was far from the death mounds of Ebensee and his life was now in his own hands, but Lou still had to ponder and hope and pray that the next day would deliver some employment and sustenance.

He admitted: "I was getting tired of knocking on those doors in Los Angeles. One more door and this was it!

But then the man who was healed back to life by Catholic nuns in Bratislava found a new deliverance by the hand of an Arab businessman also encountered in Los Angeles with a real opportunity for Lou in nearby San Diego. "Ironically, I met him on Los Angeles Street! That was where all the jobbers were located, one after the other. They were all in the wholesale business." Lou explained that Yufe was doing trade in San Diego and now this new sympathizer would recognize Lou's goodness and also help him.

"His name was Nassif Ellis. He was the owner of the place where I got credit. Some of his family is still around. We became good friends. So I told him my story, that I'd like to buy some merchandise to peddle but I don't have any money. So he said, 'All right, go and pick out what you want.' So I did. He sat with me and calculated the figures, the bottom line so I could work with him. And he said to me, 'If you give me half, I will trust you for the other half.' I said to him, 'Mr. Ellis, the situation did not change since I walked in here and told you that I don't have any money.' He said, 'Did you ever do any peddling before?' I answered him no and I was inexperienced. He said, 'Then what happens if you go broke? How will you pay me?' I said, 'Mr. Ellis, if I go broke, I will sweep your sidewalks, clean your toilets, whatever it takes. You will get paid. It may take a long time for me to pay you, but you will get paid.'"

When Lou Dunst speaks, there is no drama. Life itself has drained him of theatrics, though not of enthusiasm and zeal. His words are wrapped in hard experience, delivered like a flowing liturgy, and utterly sincere. There is a quiet strength in him, an emotional piety that is separate from his synagogue devotions. In a sense, he has nothing to lose that he hasn't already lost, so why would he patronize you with artificiality and nonsense? His promises are as hard-core as his laughter; the man is completely irresistible because you know that he is utterly incapable of not meaning what he says. He has conquered brutality with the power of truth.

So, as for Nassif Ellis, Lou reports: "He listened to me and he said, 'You know what? I am going to trust you.' And he did."

Yufe and Lou shared an apartment together in those early days in San Diego. "He did very well in peddling and I did so-so. His son, the one that fought for Israel, came over and he had me translate letters and address envelopes from Yiddish." Lou recalls this matter-of-factly, without fanfare; for Lou there are no celebrities or personages. Everybody struggles equally and craves love in the same way.

I remarked to Lou that his life after the war was a series of fortuitous happenings that all guided him along a providential path. He responded, as he often does, with his expression, "the branches,"—as though he regards his life as a tree. "Branches here, branches there: everywhere branches of things that were happening. A million branches!" Lou smiled effusively, the light of his face for a moment drenching the darkness of his deepest memories with elation and gratitude and an uncanny optimism.

"Nobody would believe this story of mine," said Lou. "I am telling it and I don't even believe it." He cites all the wondrous things, the surviving of the kingdom of death, the discovery of his sister, the transit through Italy to Canada and then to the United States; the recovery from a near-fatal collision near Lakeland, Florida and the improbable discovery of Yufe; the quirk of fate that tied him to Nassif Ellis and his own eventual, stellar success as a businessman—all of these he connects to God. "They are all miracles," he states simply and faithfully.

And then in San Diego there came the miracle of Estelle.

CHAPTER FIFTEEN

"It was time for Lou to have a birthday"

OU DUNST MET HIS FUTURE WIFE AT THE JEWISH COMMUNITY Center. He was establishing a financial foothold in the community and doing well enough socially to have been elected as president of the San Diego Jewish Singles Club. While the memories—and significant nightmares of the boxcars and the death camps—haunted and disturbed his sleep, he made the best of every day. He worked with zest and thankfulness; he mixed with people enthusiastically, even while keeping a protective veil over the inexplicable and psychologically mutilating years that he had somehow survived.

He was not yet telling his story—that would come later. He just wanted to lead a life that had a semblance of order, logic, and normality. And he welcomed the opportunity to meet a nice woman.

It was not so unusual in those primal days of the now expansive San Diego Jewish community, when immigrants from colder, wetter parts of the continent were beginning to arrive for the relief of faithful sunshine and pleasing ocean breezes. There was a pool table at the Center and she was a pretty good player. It was while she was playing with two fellows that a mutual friend came up with Lou. Yet Estelle Addleson was unusual: clear-eyed, feisty, direct, with a mind of her own. She was also as striking in appearance as she was outspoken in demeanor. But above all in terms of being atypical, she was a native of San Diego. Nevertheless, she was (and remains), in her own words, "someone often mistaken for a 'pushy New Yorker.'"

"Yes," she told me, her eyes blazing with love for her husband of decades, "I was just about to make a great shot—had the billiards lined perfectly—and here is this man, and he wants to talk to me. I wasn't all that interested in him, I was intended on making a good shot. And I did!"

Her perceptions changed; she soon discovered a gentleman that she describes as "deep, very deep." The free-wheeling and opinionated woman from the solar California coast was touched and affected by the circumspect and emotionally-guarded man from the dark ravines of Eastern Europe.

"He is a unique man," she told me. "He has taken this tragedy and turned it around to a benefit. And he can recall things with humor. Some of the worst situations—he reasons things out, somehow. It all goes back to his teachings and his values. He quotes the Torah. He so loves the Torah—and he knows what's in it. He's always teaching me something from it. I'm getting a second lesson from him."

Estelle esteems the humility that Lou displays and evokes in every category. "Some people who know the Torah teach it to you but they make you feel like you're dumb. He shares it with love and passion and he just makes you feel warm about the whole thing."

Did God choose Lou Dunst to live?

"Yes, I do believe that," said Estelle. "He made a promise to God. Like Lou says, he didn't have anybody to talk to. If he talked to another inmate and said he was cold, the other person would say he was also cold. If he said he was hungry, the other one would say he was hungry, too. So Lou could only talk to God. So he made a promise to God and he's keeping his promise."

Estelle specified that Lou keeps his vow two or three times a week—addressing groups in the community and around the nation and telling the story. It is clear to her that this commitment is therapeutic for Lou although it is profoundly redemptive for her husband as well. It's his part of the bargain that he made with Ha-Shem: the narrative for his life; the history so there might be a future.

And yet: Lou has many restless nights. "He tosses and turns, struggling with the nightmares that have plagued him since those times." She is awakened by his muffled cries, his physical shuddering, as he is swept into images and sounds of torture, sodomy, machine gun fire, splattered blood, piled corpses. In his sleep, he again suffers his belly's starvation, he smells the stench of deprivation, his soul is ripped by the rusty barbed wire of the terrible and endless European night.

Estelle speaks of these nocturnal traumas with empathy and eloquence. She's reporting an intensely distressing pattern of travail and irresolution, a chronic web of unforgiving strain that plagues her husband's psyche and gnaws at his ability to lead a genuinely peaceful life. On the outside, you see a cheerful man with a love of life and a ready wit. But the only beings who have any inkling of what hurts inside Lou Dunst are God, Estelle, and Lou himself.

The occasion to publicly share his angst and chronicle came by accident.

Estelle reminisced that years ago, Lou was engaged in an informal discussion with some friends and acquaintances. Uncharacteristically at that time, he mentioned that he is a Holocaust survivor—which got their attention and curiosity. He told them, "Ask me anything you want, there are no boundaries, the sky's the limit, and I'll answer anything."

Lou's soul had suddenly opened and he found the language of redemption. Estelle said, "And I could see that he had to start telling the story. This is when I did a push."

Estelle then recalled that she and Lou went to the synagogue on the eve of Yom Ha-Shoah—the annual Holocaust Remembrance Day. "They asked for survivors to come up and light the candles," Estelle recalled. Then her righteous indignation flared up:

"Do you know that they never called upon him?"

Estelle, her voice quivering, pointed out that a child was called up to light a candle for her grandmother who had perished. "I was incensed," she said. "I could see the disappointment on Lou's face. But he wouldn't say anything."

Estelle certainly did, however. The oversight was addressed and redressed. Estelle, nursing her husband's disappointment, sensing his need—but even more so fighting for the educational values he could bring to the discussion—challenged the synagogue's senior staff members to contact Lou and ask him to teach, to tell his story.

"That's how it all got started," she declared proudly.

Lou Dunst, though coping with his memories day and night, would now find a way to distill them in favor of light and learning and hope. His informal, not-for-profit career as an inspirational speaker (each and every time he receives a gift or donation for one of his appearances, he assiduously chooses a charity to re-direct the funds to) began and it has continued for decades and across continents.

There are innumerable agencies, high schools, colleges, and communal institutions to which he returns annually and he is unfailingly received with affection, awe, and respect. From judges to juvenile delinquents, from nuns to Navy Seals, from rabbis to reverends, Lou Dunst is sought out for his history, his humility, and his humor. He has a personal archive of adoring and articulate and grateful letters that ranges in the thousands upon thousands. "These letters," said Estelle, "encourage him. "From the students, the various individuals who are there, the judges, and the military people that he has helped in their struggles with isolation and fear and such things."

He has changed people's lives, reversed their biases, and softened their hearts. He has fulfilled his bargain with God and he converted ashes to love.

At one point in our ongoing dialogue during the year 2013, Lou told me that he wasn't a hundred percent certain what definitive date is his birthday. He knows that he was born in 1926 and he has a rough idea about when but, as he says, "We didn't make a fuss about birthdays, like people do now." There was no doubt, however, that Lou spent eighty years on earth without having a birthday party—such rituals were unknown in his childhood environment and hardly a part of life for him in the ensuing years.

When his eightieth year approached, it was Estelle who declared to a few close friends, "It is time for Lou to have a birthday." The result—a total surprise for the modest storyteller—was historic enough to be widely covered in the media: It was on the front page of the *San Diego Union-Tribune*, and a feature on four TV stations in San Diego. It was also covered by two editions of the *Los Angeles Times*.

THE WHITE HOUSE
WASHINGTON, DC 20500 SOUTHERN MD 207

08 MAR 2006 PM 4 T

Ms. Lou Dunst
3635 Seventh Avenue, 13D
San Diego, California 92103

THE WHITE HOUSE
WASHINGTON

Happy Birthday! May your special day be one of joy, and may your future be filled with the love of family and friends.

With best wishes on this special occasion,

A lavish canopy of balloons in the ballroom of the San Diego Mission Valley Doubletree Hotel framed a banner announcing LOU's 80th. It was March 5, 2006—just short of sixty-one years after Staff Sgt. Robert Persinger broke through the gates of Ebensee in the "Lady Luck" tank and liberated the death camp.

The ballroom was festive and colorful. Instead of flowers, a large chocolate floral arrangement was the edible center piece of each table. The chocolate pieces had childhood pictures of Lou, Irving and Risi. These original pictures were found in the New York apartment of the cousin who came to Jasina in 1932 to study medicine in Vienna. On the back of each chair was a gift tote bag with a picture of Lou flanked by two good-looking female judges with the US Supreme Court chambers in the background. Each bag was entitled "Lou and the Benchbabes, Lou's 80th."

Hostess Estelle Dunst introduced the cause of the party and that the M.C. would be Judge Janet Berry from Reno, Nevada presiding, and called upon Federal Judge Norbert Ehrenfreund who gave a dramatic introduction of Robert Persinger. Also present was Irving Dunst, Lou's brother, who located the dying Lou on May 6, 1945, and had him ferried to safety via the arriving GI's, was very enthused to be there and didn't have a clue that he would also be a part of the program. Lou Dunst, in his special blue yarmulke, looked pleased and jubilant, and he looked around and recognized so many familiar faces, people that he hadn't seen for many years; all present for Lou.

It was a gathering unlike any convened before at the Mission Valley Double Tree. Family and friends had flown in from all over the country. It would be the only time that Irving Dunst would ever speak about the Holocaust. His sons learned of their father's experiences for the first time at the party. He never spoke before; they never knew of his earlier years of hell. There was Irving's second wife, Alice, and Irving's adult children and grandchildren—each of their lives a triumph over The Final Solution. Irving's first wife, Magda, died on the day of their 50th anniversary.

There was Risi's daughter, Judy with her husband Ted—personifying the defiance of a new Jewish generation that would not succumb, as Risi did, to the shadows and depressions of the postwar wreckage. Hebrew blessings were spoken, and led by Lou. Israel regaled, yarmulkes worn—each act a defiance of what the Nazis had intended and that they failed to fulfill. Risi did not attend as she was gravely ill and died two weeks later.

In the months before the event, the determined and meticulous Estelle had undertaken a very special search: she was going to find the soldier who liberated her husband and bring that man to this gathering as a surprise. It must be remembered that Lou had never met Bob Persinger. He knew of him, and what the soldier had done. He had thanked him in his own heart every day but they had never crossed paths but for the convolution of history and fate. Sixty years after the deliverance, relying on news reports, military documents, and the Internet, Estelle found Persinger: he was a retired salesman living in Rockford, Illinois. Estelle arranged to fly the veteran to San Diego; Persinger graciously and gratefully acceded and happily conspired to keep the reunion a secret until he was introduced a half-hour into the proceedings.

Nobody who was there will ever forget the moment when the lanky, jaunty Sgt. Persinger, natty in his suit, appeared from the back of the hall, walked up to the podium like a sentinel and grasped the completely overcome Lou Dunst:

> The 250 members of the audience gasped in emotion and prayer. Lou, always reserved, eternally dignified, was unable to contain himself. Both men were visibly shaken and teary. The several enduring moments of silence and awe proved more eloquent than any of the day's speeches.

The press table, set up by Estelle, with reporters and videographers representing all the regional media as well as correspondents from the *Los Angeles Times*, was hushed for a beat. These journalists had all seen a lot, but they had not witnessed something quite like this. After Robert Persinger spoke about his experiences at the end of the war, and how these things had shaped his vision and morality, Lou responded with his hallmark simple dignity: "Sgt. Persinger, thank you for saving our lives."

The birthday celebration continued. The morning brunch was for family and friends, and the evening dinner was for the immediate family and several close friends to meet personally with Robert Persinger. They had the opportunity to ask any questions and fill in many gaps with this wondrous former GI. This is when Irving truly opened up and was able to have closure. Irving rarely initiated conversations; he was not unfriendly, merely sort of shy. But that night he approached Estelle and placed a hand on each shoulder and said: "Estelle, you should have a big star on each shoulder, I am so impressed with the day's activities". She will never forget this: it was the ultimate compliment. When Estelle went to pay for the dinner she was told that it had already been taken of — by Irving!!

The San Diego Mayor Jerry Sanders sent a proclamation declaring Lou Dunst Day; the Assistant Attorney General for California, Howard Wayne, sent a letter to his friend Lou Dunst; the US Judicial College presented a plaque honoring Lou; there were messages from County, State and Federal offices congratulating Lou; and a birthday greeting card from the White House signed by President George and Laura Bush was read.

Some seven years after this historic occasion, I sat with Lou Dunst, as we often did, in San Diego's renowned "Jewish deli," D.Z. Akin's. As always, he was focused yet accessible, contemplative, and thoroughly pleased to be there. The din of chirping people, cash registers, and canned music did not distract him from being mindful of his guest's every need, respectful at every appearance of our server and her steaming pot of coffee, grateful for just being alive. Even in a busy restaurant, Lou had the bearing of a living Torah scroll and the good manners of a man who sees the reflection of God's work in every person. It is often mockingly remarked about some prominent teachers of social justice: "Loves humanity, hates people." Not so Lou Dunst. Lou reveres humanity and he adores people.

Lou was reflective: His mind was back in the boxcars—the ghastly transports of terror, confinement, starvation, thirst, and bubbling human waste. It seemed to me that Lou regarded these death trains as the vehicular equivalents of any concentration camp. He was talking about survival and faith.

"When I speak to people, they want to know if, when I was going through the boxcars and everything else, what I thought about God. Did I believe in God, did I forsake God? Or, where is God, they ask me. My feeling was that *Ha-Shem* is always there. No matter what the situation. Even in the gas chamber, when we were in Mauthausen, inside I felt that *Ha-Shem* can hear me. He must be here! There is no way I would exclude Him—what good would that do me? He's going to help us! And He did!"

Lou took a deep breath and smiled. "This was all proven to me. I am here. I am alive."

Another breath, as if each breath is a portion of heaven.

"I don't have the abilities to have done the things that I have done. Surviving, coming here, and succeeding in business. I am uneducated. I don't have that many skills. How did this all happen? *Ha-Shem.* There's no other way to explain it and this I carry with me every moment of my life."

A few moments passed. The survivor and I sipped on coffee and took in our friendship. Then, quietly, Lou said: "I miss them. I miss my parents. I remember the old days. We were a close family. Everybody took care of everybody else. There was no such thing as 'I'm doing my own thing.' So I guess I keep thinking about what, well, what it might have been like if things were different. If the Nazis hadn't come...

"I think I keep looking for something. But I don't know what it is that I'm looking for."

He does know, this Lou Dunst. He does—it's just that it only becomes clear to him when he has someone nearby to listen.

LOU DUNST MAUTHAUSEN'S NUMBER 68122 THAT WAS DONATED TO THE
UNITED STATES HOLOCAUST MUSEUM IN WASHINGTON, D.C.

AFTERWORD

Lou's Love of Life's Moral Values
BY ALBERTO HAMUI

I MET LOU DUNST ON A SATURDAY MORNING SOMETIME DURING THE year 2010. Having lunch after the Shabbat services in the synagogue, a friend of mine pointed to a man sitting with us at the same table. "Do you know Lou?" He asked. "No, nice meeting you, my name is Alberto," I responded. And we started talking to each other, as if no one else was at the table or in the room; like we had known each other for years. We talked for more than an hour, until he had to leave.

Later on I reflected about what had happened to me during that meeting. This kind and soft-spoken individual had an aura that radiated a positive energy. It made me feel peaceful and calm—inviting me to connect with him.

So, what about these feelings? "Who is this guy?" I asked my friend Ruben. "His name is Lou Dunst, he is a member of the synagogue and he is a Holocaust Survivor." My interest in Lou kept growing as we started to talk every Shabbat in the synagogue; soon we developed a deep friendship.

He told me about his years in the concentration and extermination camps. Auschwitz-Birkenau, Mauthausen and Ebensee. It was at those camps that Lou Dunst talked to, and heard from God. I was moved and his life was felt by my soul. As he spoke about it, the need for memorializing his story was increasing. Somebody should write The Book about the life of Lou Dunst!

Yes, a book about how Lou Dunst, who after surviving the darkest moments of his life, was able to turn it around 180 degrees. From literally living in hell; from meeting Death face to face; from watching his parents vanishing and turning into ashes together with millions of Jews, men women and children; to a life full of love, compassion and good deeds. He turned violence into peace, enemies into friends and hate into love.

His love of God together with the unconditional love and support for every human being breaks all barriers of religion, race, social class, skin color, appearance, or sexual orientation.

It is not only his great love that impressed me, but also the absence of hate. His Jewish moral values never vanished. The giant nazi[27] criminal machine couldn't burn those values, or gas them, or machine gun them, or starve them to death. Lou's values stayed with him as a rock, as tall and firm as the tallest peak in his native Carpathian Mountains. Lou often says when he is asked about this issue: "The Jewish people don't only survive the nazis; we buried them. And we will bury all those that try to harm us."

Lou Dunst was sitting in his balcony overlooking the San Diego Bay and the park below one warm spring morning. He saw the brightness of the blue sky merging with the ocean's blue waters in the distance and transitioning with the different green colors at Balboa Park, going from bright emerald to pale green. He was breathing the clean and soft air brought on by the light ocean breeze. "Ah!" he said to himself with an expression of gratitude, "we live in the best place in the world. This is a God's gift that cannot be matched".

While *being grateful for every breath he was taking*,[28] that old familiar musty, damp unbearable smell passed through his mind, and brought him back seventy years ago to those memories when he was grasping for some fresh air. He remembered when he was transported, packed together with hundreds and thousands other Jews, in those box-cars with little air to gasp for on a one-way destination and no coming back. There was no food, water, or sanitary facilities.

A human being may live without food and water for several days and may even survive the sickness and complications of the unsanitary conditions. But it cannot survive without air for even a few minutes. And there was very little air in those box cars, in the Auschwitz gas chambers or in the Ebensee pile of corpses. And even then Lou says, *"I was grateful to God for every breath taken."*

Lou feels God's presence all the time, everywhere, day and night. "And, yes, God was with me in the box cars, in the concentration camps, in the gas chambers and even in the crematoria. *God was always with me and I never lost faith.* He was the source of the air for me during all those horrible moments. I talked to Him regularly, even when I wanted to commit suicide. He told me that I was going to break one of His Ten Commandments, *"Thou shall not kill."* Lou asked again to be saved, and was given another opportunity to live, so he can tell the story of the biggest mass murder catastrophe in the history of mankind. *Lou never gave up* and may be that was the reason that his life was spared.

---

27   I refuse to refer to them with a capital letter. They don't deserve it.
28   The texts in red are intended to be a reader's guide to Lou's Life Moral Values.

All the inmates around him, the Jews, the gypsies, the Russian prisoners of war, the homosexuals and also the crippled, *were all God's children.* A high school girl asked a question during one of Lou's recent talks: "Did you get anything positive from the concentration and death camps?"

Lou replied emphatically: "There is a very positive and important lesson I learned while sharing the living hell with my fellow inmates. *They were all brothers and sisters, regardless of religion, race, creed or appearance.* I respected everyone then, now, and I will continue to respect everybody for the rest of my life. *Always be kind to others—always.* They are all our brothers and sisters."

"*Removing all hate from your heart and filling it with love* is also a positive, especially after seeing so much hate, pain and killings." Lou added. "If there is hate in you, there is no room for love. Get rid of any kind of hate you might have, either conscious or not, big or small, open or hidden. You should have only love in your heart. That's what I did, for my own sake, otherwise I would have died," he emphasized. "That alone shall bring you comfort and happiness. *Try to choose happiness and maintain a good sense of humor.*"

Going back to his balcony in San Diego, he realized that, being a Saturday afternoon, it was time to *study the Torah.* Lou went inside to his studio to grab a *Chumash* —one of his many Jewish books that contains the five books of Moses— then went back and sat in the front of the balcony. As he was looking for the portion of the week to be read, his mind went back to Jasina, his childhood town.

It was in his early years when little Lu-Lu first *studied, and then followed the teachings of the Torah.* He did it then, he is doing it now and he will continue to follow them for the rest of his life. He learned it by example in the everyday life of his father Mordecai, his mother Priva, his sister Risi and his brother Yitzhak. And also by attending the *cheyder* with his teacher "*Zeyde*" Schnek

Little Lu-Lu learned all the 613 *Mitzvot* –good deeds- contained in the Torah. He learned about, and *celebrated every Shabbat* as it is mandated: *It is a day for peace.* Everybody needs at least one day a week to rest. Use it for meditation, for spirituality, for peace and quiet. Every Friday afternoon, in preparation for the incoming Shabbat, the daily life in Jasina stopped: there was no business, no traveling and no school.

This past week was particularly hectic for Lou. So, when the Shabbat started with the Friday's sunset, he embraced it not only spiritually, but physically. He really needed the rest and the peace it brings to the spirit. In the morning he attended the Shabbat services at a nearby synagogue and afterwards, we enjoyed our dear and mutual company during a two hour lunch. We were discussing a variety of topics. These ranged from human behavior to God's actions, to distant memories, to mundane themes. But one of them came up vividly, it was *Education.*

As Lou pointed out and emphasized it, this is an essential part of every human being: *Education, Education and Education.* Lou was kicked out of school when he was 11 years old, for the simplest reason of just being a Jew; his education was truncated by the nazis. But he has sought education at night schools in Rome and Toronto, at Sunday schools, and at every corner of his life. As I have often pointed out, Lou has a Masters' degree from one of the best "Ivy League" schools in the country: the "University of Life."

Lou's knowledge about life and death, about morality and ethics, about love and hate, about humanity, about everyday life's values, compares with very few people in the face of the earth. *Lou's education and values* are beyond description. He is a walking moral encyclopedia, a "live Google search engine" of human behavior. You can write that the love in his heart is larger than the Library of Congress.

Lou doesn't have an email address account, he doesn't know how to operate a computer, and he is not a member of any modern virtual social network. But all his values, actions and good deeds here on earth, are tabulated into his *Mitzvah Account* in heaven; its numbers are bigger than Facebook, Twitter, Apple and Microsoft members combined.

When I asked Lou the meaning of the two Hebrew words חֲזַק וֶאֱמָץ (*Hazak ve'Ematz*) that he often mentions to me, Lou responded with some trepidation in his voice: "Strength and Courage. That is what Moses told Joshua while transferring the Command of the Jewish People before entering the Promised Land."

Beautiful, but not enough. There should be something else that Lou is not telling me. My first thought was that more research needed to be done about it. I consulted with Rabbi Attia, and found that those words חֲזַק וֶאֱמָץ were actually coming from Ha-Shem to Joshua in the following passage:

> "Only the very **strong and courageous** to observe and fulfill in
> accordance with all of the teaching commanded to you by Moses
> my servant, do not stray from it neither to the right or to the

left, in order that you will be successful in all of your endeavors."
(Joshua 1:7)

As it happens that Rabbi Attia is also a *Soffer* (a person that is allowed, and
has the skills, to write the letters of the Torah in accordance with all the rules
and traditions of the Jewish People), he was engaged to reproduce that full
passage especially for Lou.

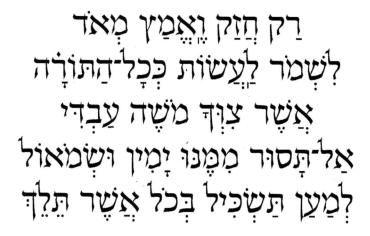

When I presented it in a wooded frame to Lou, he immediately asked, "Where
did you get this from?" So he heard the story about Soffer Attia and his eyes
started to get wet and may be one or two drops were sliding down his cheeks
reflecting the bright sun of the morning. That was a sign to me that there was
something more about "*Hazak ve'Ematz.*"

Sure enough, his wife Estelle sent me an email that same night telling the
full story: Back in his early years, Lou had very good friends in Jasina, probably
his best friends ever. Whenever they met each other they didn't say hello or
shalom. They said to each other "*Hazak ve'Ematz.*" That was their salutation.

They were dreaming of going to Palestine, the Promised Land, before it
became *Eretz Israel*. They were dreaming of fighting the British and opening
the borders to every Jewish person that wanted to flee Europe and *establish
what today is known as the State of Israel.* To offer freedom to every Jewish
man, woman and child; to be citizens of a free and democratic country of their
fellow Jews; to have a future for themselves and for future generations; *to have
a country with secured borders*; in one sentence: to be human beings again. "If

we had a country with secure borders at the time, we wouldn't have our ashes being spread over Europe", he once said.

Yes, those were the dreams of Lou and his friends. Instead, he witnessed how, one by one, all of his friends vanished in Auschwitz.

Lou never used those two words again for more than 60 years until his later years in San Diego, California. So when he received those framed words just outside the synagogue, it was understood that his tears, sparkling like diamonds, were a tribute to the memory of the souls of his childhood friends. Today that passage is hanging on a prominent wall in Estelle and Lou's apartment.

Earning a living and staying in business in San Diego has been very difficult for most of Lou's life. He started as a peddler in 1954. A few years later he opened a tiny little store in the Barrio Logan and within some years he grew it into a department store. He closed it down after 30 years.

He was successful, and always *fair in his business dealings.* He always tried to give the customer a *little more than what they paid for.* Also, the treatment of the people that worked for him was always more than fair. "When I liquidated the store and the last person I had to let go was my secretary of 30 years, we both cried that day. I kept sending her an annual bonus for many years until she died".

With the little extra money that Lou was making from the store, he started to invest in real estate. He bought a duplex and rented it out, and then another, and soon a small apartment building. "I became a silent partner with some very good and honest people that knew what they were doing. They sold the properties and I reinvested the proceeds with them. They were the experts, not me. I reinvested again and again. I didn't know how but I started to be very successful."

Soon there were some friends and people that needed some money, so he lent it to them. *The loans were with no interest and no maturity date.* At the same time, *"I helped and supported the community."* Lou has always participated in any major project of the three different synagogues that he and Estelle belong to, and has been a major donor to non-Jewish causes as well.

Lou has helped the needy people since he was a free person. His goal is to *help the needy without telling anybody* and if it is possible *not even to the individual being helped.* He has done it in the past, he is doing it now, and he will continue doing it during the rest of his life. He also has established several funds to *help the needy and the poor.* He personally *offers moral support to the individuals in their moments of darkness.* **Being** *tolerant and patient to others* gives Lou the opportunity to see inside the people around him. He will *never hurt any human being feelings, nor will he shame anybody under any circumstances.*

Almost a year after the passing of his brother Irving, Lou is still moved and sad from the pain of losing him. The relationship between them went beyond being brothers. They were the only two human beings who knew and understood each other, knew of their unbelievable circumstances of their survival, how they helped each other and were finally able to live as free human beings and both achieve success in their chosen ventures.

"They spoke on the phone once or twice a day: Irving in Los Angeles and Lou in San Diego. It was such an automatic gesture that even to this days Lou finds himself reaching for the phone to call Irving," Estelle recalls. "The loss is beyond explanation." Irving was not the extrovert that Lou is. His wife Magda was very social, so he went along with her many plans and parties and enjoyed them all.

On the other hand Lou is very extroverted, very friendly, and a good mingler. He is always engaged in a conversation. Lou is up on the daily news, reads the entire newspaper daily and falls asleep with a book every night. While driving he has the radio news on—doesn't miss a beat.

One of his great attributes is his honesty: he will not lie; not even a white one! Lou doesn't know how and he refuses to learn. He either tells the truth or avoids any comment. *"And greatest of all is his loyalty,"* Estelle remarks. "Lou's friendship is golden. He has a 24 hours open line and will do anything for a friend; his wallet is always open."

He always says no to violence and does not have an ounce of hate in his body; rather he radiates love and kindness. He has been blessed with the spiritual light from *Ha-Shem*. A group of ladies, represented by Dol Cole and Ginger Baldwin, wrote after one of Lou's talks in Del Mar, CA: "You have the light within you that shines and can never be extinguished".

This light within makes him able to attract goodness all around him. Otherwise how do you explain that there have been all these good people around him, not known to him until a few years ago?

Professional men and women alike are gratefully offering him, help, ideas, hard work and services. They refuse to accept any money. Their only compensation is the knowledge and the feeling of blessing that comes with be associated with Lou. Lou has repeatedly told each of them: "I am speechless and I really appreciate it from the bottom of my heart. May God bless you and your family."

It is indeed a blessing and at the same time a great *Mitzvah* to be next to him and to help him spread *his message of Love* and *inspire* the present, and future generations *of brothers and sisters.*

Back on the balcony Lou perceived that the positive energy and the spirituality of the Shabbat were slowly coming to an end as the sun was turning red at sunset. The blue sky changed to orange, and a few minutes later it was dark, only to be illuminated by the tiny white stars and a lovely moon wanting to grow. "That was another day, and it was good". Lou said. "Let's wait to see what God is sending His children for tomorrow...."

PHOTO GALLERY

LEFT: LOU'S FATHER WITH BICYCLE. RIGHT: LOU'S MOTHER AND FATHER

LEFT: IRVING. RIGHT: RISI AND LOU.

LEFT: RISI WITH NEW YORK COUSIN HELEN. RIGHT: LOU AND UNCLE ABRAHAM.

AUNT ESTHER, PRIVA, GRANDFATHER ISRAEL,
UNCLE ABRAHAM, COUSINS IRA AND RISI.

LOU AND CHILDREN OUTSIDE SCHOOL.

JASINA RESIDENTS, 1930s.

BROTHER IRVING AND MAGDA'S WEDDING, ISRAEL,1949.

LEFT: LOU SPEAKING AT CHURCH FOR YOM HASHOAH. RIGHT: LOU PRAYING.

SOFFER ATTIA AND HELAINE GREEN WITH RESTORED TORAH.

ALBERTO AND LOU, SHABBAT DINNER 2012.

LOU AND ESTELLE DUNST.

PREVIOUSLY BY BEN KAMIN

STONES IN THE SOUL: One Day in the Life of an American Rabbi (Macmillan, 1990)

RAISING A THOUGHTFUL TEENAGER: A Book of Answers and Values for Parents (Dutton, 1996), paperback edition, 1997.

THINKING PASSOVER: A Rabbi's Guide to Holiday Values (Dutton, 1997)

THE PATH OF THE SOUL: Making Peace With Mortality (Dutton/Plume, 1999)

REMORA: A Novel of the Rabbinate (Dorrance, 2007)

THE SPIRIT BEHIND THE NEWS: Finding God in Family, Presidents, Baseball, Cell Phones, and Chevy Impalas (Muffin Dog Press, 2009)

NOTHING LIKE SUNSHINE: A Story in the Aftermath of MLK Assassination (Michigan State University Press, 2010).

ROOM 306: The National Story of the Lorraine Motel (Michigan State University Press, 2012)

DANGEROUS FRIENDSHIP: Stanley Levison, Martin Luther King Jr., and the Kennedy Brothers (Michigan State University Press, pending for 2014)